The Absence of a Life

✦

Edwin Ross Elliott 1893-1935

Janet Lloyd

For Chris,
a blessed presence
with thanks,
Janet Lloyd

iUniverse, Inc.
New York Bloomington

The Absence of a Life

Edwin Ross Elliott 1893-1935

iUniverse books may be ordered through booksellers or by contacting:

iUniverse
1663 Liberty Drive
Bloomington, IN 47403
www.iuniverse.com
1-800-Authors (1-800-288-4677)

ISBN: 978-0-595-51054-2 (pbk)
ISBN: 978-0-595-61748-7 (ebk)

Printed in the United States of America

iUniverse rev. date: 11/4/2008

To my family and their gifts of presence in my life.

To my husband, Bill; our sons and daughters-in-law, Mark and Jeri, Phil and Karen, Andy and Pam, John and Laura; and our grandchildren, Sarah, Ian, David, Geoff, Nathan, and Daniel.

Special credit for writing the book goes to Jeri Lloyd, its first reader and editor, and to Mark and Laura Lloyd, who reproduced and arranged the photographs.

To Doris Nordstrom and my Telos writing class at Bellevue Community College, who, week after week, encouraged and inspired me as I wrote.

To the Ignatian SEEL community in Seattle. On the retreat days, this book began to come together.

To the late Ira Progoff, who introduced me to his Intensive Journal.

To the late and beloved Madeleine L'Engle, noted writer, theologian, and teacher, in thanksgiving for the special magic in her writing workshops.

To Saint Margaret's Episcopal Church, Bellevue, Washington, particularly the Healing Ministers and Stephen Ministers. For over forty years, my spiritual home.

And most especially, to the Reverend Wally Bristol, pastor, priest, confessor, and friend, who first asked the question, "Do you ever talk to your father?"

Prologue

In March 2003, I was nearly seventy years old, and it was my first trip to Hawaii. I went to the delightful island of Maui with my husband, Bill.

Each day, we watched whales jumping and arching not far from shore and reveled in exquisite sunsets. We listened to the sound of a conch shell being blown on the beach, attended a luau, and took walks and drives to enjoy beautiful scenery.

But I wanted to go snorkeling. I couldn't explain this strange longing. I have what I take to be a reasonable fear of deep water. Although I enjoy my water aerobics class in shallow water, I can barely swim across our neighborhood pool at home. Somehow, I wanted to snorkel, not in the shallow waves near the shore, but from a boat out on the ocean.

So off we went. From the busy dock at the town of Lahaina, we boarded an excursion boat that took tourists out on the ocean to find the best places to snorkel. Bill may have thought I would abandon the snorkeling idea when I was confronted with the reality of deep ocean water. We cruised straight out from shore for a long time. I pasted a confident look on my face, trying to emulate and impress the other passengers, but soon I felt numb. Even the butterflies in my stomach had turned numb. Finally the boat stopped. The crew had found a snorkeling spot, and it was time to do it.

We were issued large rubber swim fins for our feet, goggles, and snorkeling masks to put over our mouths and noses. A tube reached upward from the masks. The tube was to stick out of the water to supply air when I snorkeled on my stomach, looking at the sea life beneath me. We were given a "noodle," which is a narrow rubber tube to put across our chests and under each arm to keep afloat in case all other maneuvers failed.

I dutifully suited up, imposing all these strange unfamiliar parts onto my already terrified body. With all the nonchalance I could muster, I managed to march across the deck without tripping on my fins and got in line to go off the boat. The line moved slowly toward the ladder where each of us climbed down into the water. To my eyes, the ocean was endless, and its depth was unfathomable. As I continued to move forward, I couldn't begin to understand why I was so determined.

When I got to the ladder, there was a father, mother, and little girl just ahead of me. The child looked to be about five years old. She was adorable in a ruffled bathing suit with the fins on her little feet. Around her waist was an inflatable plastic donut, decorated with Disney figures, much like one a child might use to splash around in a swimming pool. Her father was already in the ocean, holding out his arms, telling her to reach out and take his hands. Her mother, beside her on the ladder, gently put her miniature goggles and snorkeling mask in place and held an arm around her as extra support while the boat bobbed up and down in the waves.

I was grateful for the delay as I stood and watched this family. The child continued to cling to her mother. Suddenly she scrambled back up the ladder.

"She isn't going to do it," the mother shook her head as she called to her husband. I watched in awe as he smiled, talked her back down the ladder, and calmly coaxed her to come to him. Finally she let go, slid off the ladder, put her hands in his hands, and they were off.

I quickly adjusted my face gear and slid off the ladder. A member of the crew tossed me a long yellow rope that was secured to the boat. Holding the rope with one hand, I moved my fins, put my head in the water, and breathed as I gazed on the multicolored tropical fish swimming below me. A turtle gave me an apprehensive look as he swam by. Soon, I had snorkeled enough and swam back to the boat, reassured by the yellow rope I clutched with a death grip. I climbed up the ladder to the familiar safety of the deck, where I looked triumphantly out onto the water.

Then I saw the little girl. She was still holding her father's hands, and she was snorkeling. Her father was smiling as he pulled her along against the waves. Her mother snorkeled beside them.

I wept, my tears blending in with the salty water running from my hair and down my face, unnoticed by others. Why was I weeping? The answer came from a deep place in my soul—along with the answer to why I was snorkeling.

I cried to myself, "My father is so proud of me."

The words rushed over me, and they came to rest forever more in my heart. You, my own father, seemed very close—such nearness I had never before experienced. I never knew you, so I may not ever be able to comprehend how proud you are. But I know we went snorkeling together in Maui. Thank you so much for making it happen.

I want to tell you my story.

Chapter 1

It's a long way back home—a very long way. It's been many years since you last held me in your arms. It's been seventy-two Christmases since you bought the special Christmas lights that twinkled on and off. You put them on our tree and sat holding me, enjoying a baby enchanted by the twinkling, multicolored lights. Christmas 1933—I've been told about this. Tragically, you died before I was two years old. This was our only magical Christmas together, with Mother, you, and me looking at our Christmas tree, a tableau, a special holy family.

I'm convinced that all mothers, fathers, and infants are holy families worthy of a Rembrandt painting. That was our golden moment. By spring, you were sick; by the next Christmas, you were in quarantine, shut away from us in the hospital. I don't remember you. I have other people's remembrances but not my own. They tell me about their lives with you. I have no life to tell. But perhaps I may. I want to tell you the story of our love and longing for connection that never goes away. I want to tell you the story of the absence of a life.

What do I call you? I didn't have words yet when you left. I am told I said da-da and knew it meant you. But perhaps others were reading into this, voicing the wishful thinking that comes from fear and dread. If I say Dad or Father, I feel angry. Others can use those words in a take-it-for-granted sort of way—"Good old Dad." Or maybe they roll their eyes as they complain, "Well, you know my father never let me do that." How I would give my life itself to be able to say those words.

This is a long journey, a very long journey, and it has just begun. It is a journey back to that Christmas and the colored twinkling lights to claim our family and our home—to claim you in my life.

Four years before you married, before you met my mother, you were a soldier in World War I. I have a picture of you in your army uniform. It was taken as your regiment marched in a parade down Second Avenue in Seattle as you left for Camp Mills on Long Island. These kinds of parades were common then. People turned out to cheer the troops going off to war. You are handsome in a still boyish sort of way.

I gaze at the picture, just as I gaze at the pictures of my four sons when they were that age. I love looking at them and remembering. They show such beauty and such vulnerability at the same time. It often brings tears to my eyes. Tears come to my eyes as I look at your picture. I see that I inherited your big ears. Your grandson John, who is thirty-nine now, inherited them as well.

How wonderful that Aunt Mae saved the letters you wrote to her and your mother during the war. No one knew what was to come and what these letters would mean later to your daughter. When I was thirteen, she gave them all to me in a large box. How precious they are—your handwriting on paper that you touched and envelopes that you licked to seal. Mother threw the box in the trash when we were packing for one of our moves. Luckily, I rescued them.

While you were at Camp Mills, you wrote about visiting New York City. You said it was so old, not shiny and new and upcoming like Seattle. You comment that it seems really on its way out. I flew to New York with your great-granddaughter, Sarah, last year to celebrate her graduation from high school. We walked the same streets that you must have walked. New York is still there.

You wrote about attending a baseball game between New York and Chicago and how much you love "ball games," as you put it. But you also wrote about drilling, marching, and artillery practice; living in a tent in the heat and humidity of a Long Island summer; eating army food; and somehow assembling an impromptu jazz band on the base. My favorite part is when you wrote that you must remember not to look up when an airplane goes over the camp or everyone will know you are a rookie. I realize that the only place you saw airplanes was at a military base.

I tell my husband and sons this story, and they laugh. We live in Seattle, and Seattle is airplane country. My husband Bill, your son-in law, worked for Boeing Airplane Company in Seattle for forty-four years. You spelled it *aeroplane*. By the way, although New York is still there, Seattle is still a shiny, new, and upcoming city.

By the time your regiment got to France, the war was nearly over, so you didn't see direct action. You wrote home that it felt like a disgrace because you wanted to return with real war stories. You hoped they wouldn't be disappointed in you. I am very sure they were not.

You wrote a lot about the people, towns, and villages in France. You made friends with a little girl in a nearby village and remarked how you miss your nieces and nephews at home. You ended with the phrase "You know, Mum, how much I enjoy being around children." You never could be with me when I was a little girl. How can you bear this? There is still a preverbal memory embedded in the cells of my body that cannot bear it either.

You were a child once as well, the sixth of nine children. You told Mother that on washing day, it was your job to turn a handle that operated the wringer on the washing machine while your mother put the clothes through it. You weren't very big, and you always had a scab on your nose from one week to the next because when you pulled the handle around it would often scrape your nose. I can picture that small boy turning that big handle. I treasure that story.

How well you wrote! How clearly you put your thoughts and feelings on paper, and your descriptions are just full of life. Where did you learn to write like this? I was told you didn't finish high school. In the farming community of central Oregon, you just stayed in school until you got too big for the desks, and then they let you go.

Others in your family were good letter writers and saved one another's letters. I have the letters Aunt Lida wrote when you were dying in the hospital. I was a young woman when I read these letters. As I read, I wept in fury at you. I didn't think you tried hard enough to live. They described your funeral. No one had ever seen so many flowers. The chapel was full and brimming over with your friends and family weeping in grief. As I read, I shrieked, "Why did you get friends and flowers and weeping and leave me behind? You didn't deserve such a tribute. You abandon a baby who couldn't even call you by name yet. You should have tried harder to live, and if you couldn't live, you should have taken me with you to die, so I could have flowers and friends and weeping too."

But in letters to Aunt Mae, Aunt Lida narrates the sequence of your final illness and death, and I was confronted with the reality of how hard you tried to get well and how hard you tried to get back to me to put those lights on another Christmas tree.

Were you frightened when you first got sick? Were you worried about us when you went to the hospital? Your beloved mother had died two years before. You two had been so very close. Did you long for her to visit you? You had to know how serious your illness was. Tuberculosis—your brother Fid died from it and so did your nephew Lester. Did you feel unbelief that this could be happening to you?

I have a letter you wrote to your sister Agnes in July, telling her how restless you felt. "A few more months of this, and I will be a mental instead of a lung case." Your words of anguish seem to jump off the page. "The doctors won't tell me anything," you complained. In this letter, you refer to me by name, telling Agnes that Mother and I are with Aunt Lida. As I read it, I realize that this is the only time I see my name written by you. It is so very precious.

Before you went into the army, you had already moved away from Terrebonne, the farming community in central Oregon where your family had homesteaded. You moved to Seattle, I think to go to business school. There you met the Campbell family and became friends with one of their sons, Bob. You and Bob joined the army at the same time, were in the same regiment, and were in France together. You were close friends for the rest of your life. When you returned, Mr. Campbell invited you to enter his business, along with Bob. J. A. Campbell Company was the name, and this small family business, sold baking equipment to wholesale bakeries. Mr. Campbell must have seen your potential. He must have seen you as very smart, outgoing, friendly, and quick to learn. You were a people person, and you must have enjoyed being a salesman. It seems like you were very good at what you did.

You met Mother in Seattle. I don't know the details, such as where or how. I have some early pictures from that time, and she was very pretty but seemed to show a reserve and shyness—a bit of not completely disguised self-consciousness. You are smiling, and you look happy and self-confident, like the world is yours.

Mother told me that when she met you she had recently come to Seattle from Mobridge, South Dakota, to work as a secretary to an executive with the railroad. Working in the railroad executive's office was a glamorous job, like working for the airlines would have been when I was a young woman. She was so good at what she did that she was transferred from Mobridge to take the job in the big city of Seattle. You married in 1922, just at the time that J. A. Campbell Company transferred you to Portland to become their regional manager.

You bought a brand-new home in Portland. Mother would talk about how you planted the yard. Mother became a homemaker and cook *par excellence*. I heard from friends and relatives how beautifully your home was furnished and decorated and what a wonderful cook she had become.

You had many friends and business associates, and she entertained magnificently. Mother belonged to several women's clubs and luncheon groups. You both played golf. Over the years, Mother often spoke of the U.C.T, the United Commercial Travelers. Apparently, this was a social organization of businessmen and their wives. She spoke of people they were acquainted with who later became very well known, such as Manning of Manning bakeries and Fred Meyer, whose first stores began in Portland. These were your heroes; young business associates of yours way back then.

I faintly remember being taken to the U.C.T. family Christmas party when I was about three, after you had died. Everyone made a fuss over me; I was such a center of attention. I didn't know what to make of it, but I loved it. I do remember being afraid of the Santa Claus. When I was supposed to sit on his lap, I ran and hid behind a curtain.

You both smoked cigarettes and served cocktails in your home. Although there was still Prohibition, you undoubtedly had your ways. This was a stretch from your early life in central Oregon, where such behavior was frowned upon.

This was your life for ten years. These were Mother's golden years. I wish I had known you both during that time, before it crumbled, before a girl child entered a world that was, even then, cracking with forebodings of the crumbling that lay ahead.

I grieve that I never knew you. I grieve that I never knew that Mother from those years either. Although she died when she was ninety and I was fifty-two, this Portland socialite was not the woman I knew, and I could never explain to her the woman I became.

I am told that you had always wanted children and that you would have been a great father. Mother was phobic about even the idea of having a child. Over the years ahead, she often told me that people who have children live in squalor forever.

"Your life is over when you have a child." She would hurl these words at me when she was in one of those states. Perhaps you can understand better than I the origin of her obsession. She was the oldest of five children, and I think she may have been traumatized by her mother's female complaints, pregnancies, and births as well as the impact of her siblings in their small home. I suspect her father played a large part in this as well. "Dad could be mean," was all that she ever said.

When she graduated from high school, she taught country school for a year in Minnesota. She said that at the end of the year, her father took all of her money. She had to teach another year and managed to keep her money that time. She then got away, went to business school, and became the self-reliant young woman she was when you met her. To the day she died, she was obsessed with social class and upward mobility. Those ten golden years were feats of accomplishment for both of you. But she couldn't understand how someone could do all of that and have a baby too.

Mother told me some sad stories of her childhood. "My younger brother George broke everything, including my dolls," she complained. "I couldn't keep anything nice." Once she saw a beautiful doll in a catalog. It looked like it had a porcelain face and body, and it was dressed in beautiful clothing. She begged and begged for the doll, knowing that if she had anything that wonderful, she would surely find a way to keep it nice.

Finally, her mother sent for it. She waited and waited for the package to come. But when it came, and she tore it open, it was the material to make an ugly cloth doll with a painted face and painted-on clothing. She was so terribly disappointed. Her mother stuffed the doll with cotton and sewed it up, but Mother had to let go of the dream of ever having the doll in that picture.

She had to cook and help around the house from an early age. Her mother seemed completely occupied with having babies and had to deal with the resulting medical complications. Mother said that when she was seven, she did the ironing with a flat iron that was heated on the stove.

The most disturbing story was when her aunt and uncle asked to adopt her sister Rene. She told me Rene was a toddler then, an adorable baby. Rene stood on the kitchen table, smiling innocently while being admired by these visitors as their mother stood by. Their mother finally decided not to let this happen, but this scene shows the financial and health issues the family must have been enduring.

Aunt Lida told me a story of my earliest beginnings. You came to her and told her Mother was pregnant. Mother was furious, distraught, and desperate about the pregnancy, and you didn't know what to do. She wouldn't yet tell anyone. Aunt Lida told the rest of your family and had a family baby shower for her. Mother finally agreed to come. In this way, I became an undeniable reality. I well remember the hot fits and cold furies Mother could have in the years that I knew her. I can picture the scene well, and I can imagine what you went through.

Mother said she couldn't bring a baby into your house because it was too small. She would need a maid—a hired girl, as they were called. So you bought a larger house and moved into it three months before I was born. This meant buying some additional furniture.

I still have a lovely desk that you bought her at that time. It is a small, cherrywood lady's desk in a French provincial style. The top folds back to reveal the slots and drawers where Mother always kept what she described as her important papers. During all the moves in subsequent years, she kept that desk. After she died, I could not bear to part with it. Refinished, it has a special place in my home.

I have a letter you wrote to your mother in 1930. You complain that your business is very slow. The country was well into the Depression by then. Was this a worry for you as it was for so many? Did buying the larger home cause more financial strain that could have contributed to your illness? Did the stress of Mother's pregnancy and my birth and Mother's resulting hysteria contribute to it as well?

Notwithstanding the stress and Mother's hysteria, I am told that you looked forward with joy to my arrival. You said I would be a red-haired girl. Your beloved mother had had red hair. After twenty-four hours of labor, which Mother talked about all of her life, I was born—a lovely, healthy red-haired baby girl. You named me Janet Marilyn.

There is a picture of you holding me when I was a tiny baby. We are outside, and you are looking down lovingly at this tiny face peering out from a snugly wrapped blanket. How I treasure this picture. Each time I look at it, I still long for your arms around me.

Mother said that I cried constantly with colic, and the diaper washing was so hard that she became exhausted. Many years later, there was an article in a newspaper about a woman who had burned down her house. When confronted, she had reported to the police that she had simply thrown a match into a pile of baby laundry and left the house. Mother laughed bitterly as she read this article aloud. With a voice of fury, she imitated what must have been the woman's tone of voice several times as she read, and then she announced that was exactly how she had felt. "That is what it is like to have a baby in the house," she exclaimed.

There is a picture of Mother holding me when I am perhaps four months old. I am smiling happily. She had that same shy tentative look I noticed in that picture early in your marriage. She is dressed in a long, formal gown with her hair beautifully done in the fashion of the day. Perhaps she is trying to recapture some sense of her former life. By that time, she was strategizing how she might fit me into her world.

I finally outgrew the colic and a hired girl appeared on the scene to wash the diapers. By the time of that magic Christmas with the twinkling lights, a new normalcy may have settled into the home. Over the years, Mother would talk of what a cute baby I was then.

She seemed to enjoy me then, to have a sense, at least in retrospect, of my specialness. Of course, all of your friends and family thought I was adorable. She got many compliments, and we all got so much attention. You said I was to be a red-haired girl, and there I was. They thought that you were magic. Through all of our moves that were to come, there are several articles of baby clothing that Mother always kept tucked away in a chest. Did they remind her of this brief, magic time when she enjoyed caring for her baby?

When you went into the hospital, Mother and I moved in with Aunt Lida, Uncle Earl, and twelve-year-old Billy. Two young women, Arlene and Faye, cousins from central Oregon, moved in with us and cared for the house and for me. Aunt Lida worked, and I think Mother was working soon as well. She was also spending as much time as possible with you at the hospital. I'm sure there must have been financial worries. It was a small house, and I had a crib in the corner of Mother's bedroom. There was no hired girl; Arlene and Faye did it all.

Aunt Lida welcomed us with open arms. Her letters from that time reflect nothing but love and acceptance and an upbeat attitude that must have kept everyone going. This early output of adoration and nurture and daily loving care, however brief it turned out to be, may hold the secret to my ultimate survival.

Mother told me that while you were in the hospital, I was baptized. Aunt Lida thought that this should happen and made arrangements at a church near their home. From what I was told, we walked to the church. There was a group of parents with babies to be baptized, but I was the only baby old enough to be walking. During the time around the font, I got loose and walked around, but apparently, I was corralled long enough for the deed to be done. Someone gave me a flower to hold. Mother must have told you about it when she came to the hospital. Were you sad that you couldn't be there? I'm sad about that too. Did you pray for me when you were sick? Did you know how much I missed you?

We moved from Aunt Lida's when I was three and began a new way of life. I am beginning to remember about this time. Mother arranged board and room with someone else in their home. The lady of the house cared for me while Mother went to work. We lived in one bedroom in these homes. Two of them were when we were still in Portland.

One family also boarded a mother who had a little boy my age. I remember that we had high chairs side-by-side in the kitchen, and we would take delight in reaching out and holding hands across the space between us, while laughing and making faces at each other. This is the earliest other child that I can remember. I had lived in an adult world.

I remember walking down the street with Mother and meeting a man. He greeted us so warmly and smiled as he picked me up in his arms.

"She looks like Ed," I heard him say to Mother.

"Did you know my Daddy?" I asked him.

"I sure did," he answered me. He and Mother talked for a bit, then he hugged me and put me down, and we moved on. I never knew who he was, but it was someone from your life, not from my life. I knew even then that my life was different. In my heart and in the cells of my body, I knew that you were gone.

I had said to the man, "Did you know my daddy?" not, "Do you know my daddy?" I had stopped looking for you. I was three and a half.

The summer I turned four, Mother and I moved to Minneapolis. I remember leaving Portland on the train. All of the relatives came to the train to see us off. There was so much hugging and kissing. I don't remember tears, but there must have been, well hidden so as not to upset me. A button came off my coat and Aunt Lida slipped a magic needle and thread from her purse and sewed it on right there on the train platform. You were gone, our home was gone, and the Oregon relatives became fading memories over the years. I was transplanted to the Midwest.

As I look back, I marvel at how much I remember of those Portland years. I am told that I talked in sentences extremely early, way before I was three. Family members called me a chatterbox, saying I "talked all the time." This ability to use language, to put words to important people and experiences, may have resulted in this very early development of my memory. It kept them real. It helped me cope with these losses as well as the losses that were ahead.

Chapter 2

"Well, well, well. Is this Jeanette?"

I remember waking from a nap to see two people standing with my mother at the foot of the bed. It was a strange bed in a strange room. I had fallen asleep in the cab on the way from the train and had been carried into the house. This was my first encounter with my Aunt Blanche and Uncle Freddy, my mother's younger sister and her husband. They would become formative in my life.

"Well, well, well. Is this Jeanette?" Freddy repeated himself as all three of them smiled indulgently at this rumple-haired little redhead who was still disoriented from sleep.

"Her name is Janet," Blanche corrected Freddy. So someone did know my name. I sat up, and they came into focus. Blanche's eyes sparkled with warmth and excitement. She wore shorts and a halter top like I wore on hot days. Did grown-ups dress like this? She was chewing gum. Freddy was tall, thin, and quiet. His straight hair was neatly combed, and he wore a suit. We had arrived in Minneapolis, the city that would be our home for the next eight years.

We stayed with Blanche and Freddy that first year in Minneapolis. Mother started her new job right away as a secretary at Russell Miller Milling Company, and Blanche was my caregiver.

Blanche was a dedicated housewife. Her home was central to her. She was a wonderful cook and an immaculate housekeeper. She dusted, scrubbed, vacuumed, and swept. She made the beds, washed the dishes, polished, and sewed. I watched her work and became familiar with her routine, which was like the daily liturgy of a monastery. She made cookies. She made me a dress.

Blanche had a vegetable garden in the backyard, and every summer day, I helped her pick green beans. Green beans were Blanche's chicken soup. If you ate enough of them, you wouldn't get sick. She piled the cooked green beans on Freddy's plate as she served dinner from the stove. I tried refusing to eat them, but Blanche said that everyone had to eat as many green beans as they were years old. So I got four on my plate that summer. Freddy's plate had so many that I knew he must be very old.

Blanche seemed to think a lot about how not to get sick. I am convinced that your sickness and untimely death affected her a great deal. I watched her serve Freddy his breakfast: always orange juice, two eggs, bacon, and two pieces of toast with butter and jam. She worried because he was too thin. He always drank a glass of milk with his breakfast. When he was absorbed in reading the newspaper during breakfast, I would see her pick up the cut-glass cream pitcher and secretly pour cream into his milk. She would gesture for me to be quiet, and I knew better than to give her away.

This was still the 1930s, during the Great Depression, and I think she also feared Freddy may not be able to work or would lose his job. I gazed at Freddy, what I could see of him above and around his newspaper. I saw him as the most precious living creature in the world, one who needed saving and protecting.

I sat quietly during this morning ritual as I waited for my breakfast, which came later, after Freddy and Mother left for work. Blanche never ate breakfast. She had a cup of coffee and a cigarette while she watched me eat. In my small-child way, I took in the undercurrents of unspoken fear.

Several times a week, Blanche and I walked to the grocery store. Blanche put her grocery money for the week in a small change purse that shut firmly by pinching together two metal clasps. After the grocer added up the total, I watched Blanche count out the money, and she carefully shut the clasps and put the change purse in a special place in her large handbag. One day, the grocer asked her if she would like to open a charge account.

"I don't believe in eating food before it is paid for," she answered emphatically.

When I grew up and began grocery shopping for my own family, I fondly remembered Blanche's change purse. I can now charge groceries using a credit card. Each time I do this, I remember Blanche and what she would have to say about that.

Blanche and Freddy never had children. Blanche told me years later that it was because she was afraid of childbirth. Her mother had told her that when you have children, it means that you lie in a pool of blood. Their mother's trauma affected Blanche as well as Mother.

There was a little girl down the street about my age named Colleen, and Blanche would invite her over to play with me. I remember how we played house and dolls and had tea parties, which included our stuffed animals, and I remember how much I enjoyed these times. Blanche knew that Colleen's father was in prison.

One day, Blanche overheard a conversation between us and she told me she held her breath as she listened.

"Where is your daddy?" I asked Colleen.

"He is far away, but we go to visit him. He is behind a fence, and we can talk to him through the fence," Colleen replied. Apparently, for me, daddies were so elusive that I accepted this and didn't press Colleen for further details. Blanche began to breathe again.

We rocked our dolls in silence for a time, and then Colleen asked, "Where is your daddy?"

There was a long pause, and I put down my doll, raised my head up high, threw out my arms, and told her, "He's up in heaven with the angels." Yes, you were somewhere too.

About that time, I remember asking to go to Sunday school. I don't know where I had heard the words. They must have had a mystical ring to them, resonating with a yearning inside of me. The word *Sunday* meant special, like Sunday best. School meant being big enough to learn. I must have kept hammering on this idea because I remember Mother and Blanche discussing this in a bewildered, what-in-the-world-should-we-do-about-this fashion. But I went. A neighbor lady picked me up and took me along with her children.

The first Christmas I can remember is the year we lived with Blanche and Freddy. Blanche loved Christmas, and, in the years to come, I often spent time with her over the holidays. Her house was decorated with familiar décor that appeared each year, assuring me that it was really Christmas.

The tree, which always went nearly to the ceiling, was covered with lights, ornaments, and tinsel. She baked cookies and fruitcakes, and the house smelled heavenly. The cut-glass candy dish, which had a cover, was filled with multicolored, hard candy. No matter how carefully I tried to put it back, the cover could be heard all over the house if I tried to sneak a piece of candy before dinner.

Blanche had a manger scene set up on a table in the living room. This included a stable with Mary, Joseph, the baby Jesus, the donkey, shepherds, wise men, sheep, and camels—and angels. Blanche must have told me the Christmas story, or perhaps I heard it in Sunday school as well. I remember telling it over and over to myself as I spent time looking at the scene. I couldn't touch anything; I could just look, but that was enough.

That Christmas Eve when we opened presents, there was a large one for me, which I had to open last. When the time finally came, I ripped it open and found a doll's trunk with a baby doll inside, cuddled in a whole wardrobe of doll clothes that Blanche had sewn by hand. How I hugged that doll.

On Christmas morning, I got up first and sat by the tree clumsily dressing and undressing her. Blanche came into the room, turned the lights on the tree, and sat on the floor to help me with the doll.

"What is her name?" Blanche asked.

"Mary Marie," I remember instantly replying. Marie was Blanche's middle name. Mary was the name of the mother in the manger scene. Mary Marie was the most beautiful name I could imagine.

"I think that's a beautiful name." Blanche smiled at me, and Mary Marie the doll became. Mary Marie was to play an important part in my ongoing history. The lights glistened on the tree—different ones, not your special twinkling ones—but true lights all the same.

Blanche took me ice-skating in Loring Park. She bought me skates with two runners on each skate, which clamped onto my shoes like roller skates. I watched Blanche glide over the ice so gracefully, impelled through space faster than I ever imagined a person could move, often skillfully weaving around the other skaters while she sped along. I would slip along, sliding one foot in front of the other as I pushed myself around on the edge of the ice. My nose ran freely over the wool scarf wrapped snuggly around my neck, and I fell about every four slides.

I would get up and do it again, over and over. I loved the skating rink, the drifts of snow piled around its edges where I stumbled along, the crisp cold, and the bare brown branches of nearby tall trees contrasted against a blue sky with a cold yellow sun. I delighted in all the skaters whizzing by me, bundled as I was against the cold in colorful snowsuits and caps, scarves, and mittens.

At last, Blanche would come over, turn in a small circle in front of me, and smile as she stopped right where she wanted to be. She picked me up, wiped my nose, and held my hand while we moved around the ice. Skating this way, I could stay upright a bit longer. Best of all, sometimes she held both of my hands and skated backwards as she pulled me along, still smiling right into my face. All too soon, we took off our skates and walked home. My legs ached, but I didn't tell her. Then we had alphabet soup for lunch.

Freddy worked for the Minneapolis branch of a Hollywood movie studio, R.K.O. Radio Pictures. He was a distributor, and it was his job to schedule the movies among the various local theaters. Freddy was a quiet person and didn't say much about his work, unless, in his mind, a very exciting movie came to town. Such was the case with *Snow White and the Seven Dwarves*.

Filming in color was a breakthrough new technology then, and an animated, full-length film with dialog, songs, colorfully crafted characters and scenes, and an intricate plot was even newer. It was hard to believe.

Freddy brought home passes for all of us to go downtown on the streetcar to the State Theater and see *Snow White and the Seven Dwarves*. I remember everyone's excitement. However, when we got there, the experience seemed strange and unreal to me. I remember being frightened, especially of the witch. I much preferred my books.

I mustn't forget to tell you how much I loved being read to. Mother often read to me in the evening before I went to bed. During the day, I looked at the pictures in the books and tried to remember the stories so I could tell them to myself over and over again. Much to my delight, by the time I heard a story read three times I had it memorized.

But being among the first to see *Snow White and the Seven Dwarves* is an exciting memory, particularly when I remember Freddy's pleasure in making this very special event happen for us. Colored animated movies were a new part of a world I was growing into that had already moved on without you.

Freddy had a home movie camera and took pictures of all of us outside in the backyard. This was unusual and special for that time. He had a projector and a screen, so later we could look at the movies. Years later, when I looked at those movies again, I noticed what a prominent role Mary Marie played in most of the shots that included me.

Freddy was a creature of habit. Nearly every evening at 9:00, he fixed himself a snack of cheese, rye bread, pretzels, and Pepsi-Cola. He sat down at the breakfast nook in the kitchen, turned on the small radio at the end of the table, and listened to Cedric Adams broadcast the news.

If I managed to keep myself awake that long, there was a chance I could join him. I would lie in bed listening to what was happening in the living room. When I heard Freddy get up and go to the kitchen, I ran to the bathroom. Mother and Blanche couldn't object to my sitting on the toilet, I thought. I perched there, leaning forward as far as I could without falling on the floor. When I heard Cedric Adam's voice, I ran for it. If I got to the kitchen table, I was safe. I scrambled up on the bench across from Freddy. Somehow, that was Freddy's territory, and I was protected.

Freddy sliced cheese for me, rich, smelly, delicious cheese—his special food. Then he gave me pretzels and a whole glass of Pepsi-Cola. Mother and Blanche would find us there, but they were helpless. Their response was the same night after night, like a Greek chorus: "Freddy, you've done it again. She should be asleep."

"She'll wet the bed."

"She's already had her teeth brushed."

"How can she eat that stuff when she didn't eat her dinner?' Freddy turned up Cedric Adams, looked down at his sandwich, smiled, and said nothing.

There was a path through the woods at the end of the backyard that led down to a nearby golf course. Sometimes there were garter snakes on the path. One day, I was walking down the path with Freddy, and I accidentally stepped on a snake before I saw it. I was wearing thin-soled, summer sandals, and I stood in horror, rigid as I felt the snake struggling under my foot. I started to scream. Freddy tried in vain to move me off the snake. I screamed louder, hysterical by this time. Finally, Freddy picked me up and carried me, still screaming, back up the path and into the house, and he turned me over to Mother and Blanche, who had rushed to the door as they heard us coming. To this day, I have a horror of snakes, even harmless garter snakes.

On weekends, I followed Freddy everywhere as he did his chores. One day, he was trying to pull some stubborn weeds from the grass and finally exclaimed, "This is a job for my long-nosed pliers." He got them from his toolbox in the garage, got a good grip on the weeds, and out they came. After that, I talked a lot about Freddy's long-nosed pliers. If there was anything that needed fixing, I piped up, "Freddy can fix it with his long-nosed pliers."

For reasons I didn't understand, Blanche thought this was hilarious, and she teased Freddy in a humorous way. "So Freddy can fix it with his long-nosed pliers, can he?" Years later, when I went to college and took Psychology 101, I learned about Freud. I fondly remembered my early fascination with Freddy's long-nosed pliers. I understood the origin of my snake phobia.

For my early, passionate, preschool self, Freddy was an overpowering, uncontrollable mystery. He was my first conscious smell of manhood. He was my lover, my surrogate daddy, my protector from a world of women, my affirmation of the realness and goodness and essentialness of a man. I pray that you know him now and may thank him.

That year, our lives seemed to settle into a familiar and reassuring pattern. But even though I don't remember it being spoken about, your death was close to the surface of our lives. One evening after dinner, it was time for my story. I couldn't find Mother. I looked everywhere and became frightened. Blanche was washing dishes, and I told her I couldn't find Mother. Blanche immediately dried her hands and went searching, with me right behind her.

In our bedroom closet, Blanche found Mother crying with her face buried in some of the clothes. She put her arm around Mother, turned to me, and said, "She's crying because she bumped her head." Red-eyed, Mother came out of the closet. She told me she couldn't read a story, but she sat on the floor with me, helping me put together one of my jigsaw puzzles. She got the pieces in wrong, but I just left them there and didn't correct her. That was the only time I ever saw Mother cry. In the years to come, she never cried. I knew she hadn't bumped her head.

One day, I remember sitting on the bench by myself at Mother's dressing table. I picked up a hairpin and began to make scratches on the surface of the dressing table. I kept making scratches for a long time. When I had scratched for a while, I thought this might be a bad thing to have done so I put my sweater over the scratches, went back to playing, and forgot all about them.

Of course, Mother found the damage and was furious. She pointed out that I had known what I was doing was wrong or I wouldn't have covered it with the sweater. She said that made it even worse. She scolded and scolded and made me sit by myself and look at the scratches for a long time and think about what I had done. She didn't come back and let me go for quite a while. I learned from that experience to be cautious about spontaneous self-expression.

Fortunately, Blanche repaired the damage. She put what must have been a wood stain over them and then used furniture polish. She rubbed very hard, and they could hardly be noticed after that. But I always could look very closely and find them. They're on the left side. Do you know that I'm left-handed?

I had my fifth birthday toward the end of that year with Blanche and Freddy. You know it is August 3. We had corn on the cob for my birthday dinner. Blanche said it was the first of the season, especially for my birthday. Drenched in butter, it was delicious. Everyone picked it up and ate it with their hands. It was a nice contrast to the green beans—on my plate were five of them.

After dinner, Mother held me on her lap, and I hugged her and started to tell her how special I felt being a big girl of five. I could feel myself getting older. She cut me off in mid-sentence and asked, "What has happened to my baby? I don't have a baby anymore." She looked at my legs, which I proudly noted reached nearly down to the floor. "What will I do?" she lamented.

I remember feeling angry, yet anxious about my anger. I wanted her to celebrate my proud five-year-old self, to be proud of it too. It felt like she was smothering it. My mother was smothering me. I knew my baby self was going away. Would Mother love me now?

I don't think you ever knew Blanche and Freddy. That's too bad because you would have liked each other so much. The confidence you might have brought to the scene could even have inspired them to have a child of their own. This would have blessed them beyond measure, and it would have been a cousin for me to play with, too.

Mother and I moved shortly after this birthday, but we always spent holidays and many Sunday dinners with Blanche and Freddy. I spent many school vacations with them. My day always ended in the kitchen with Freddy and Cedric Adams. Their house is my memory of a real home. To this day, I smile when I catch myself keeping house or cooking in a way reminiscent of Blanche. I feel a pang of guilt when I charge groceries. I still have corn on the cob on my birthday, and the green beans on my plate increase faithfully every year.

Chapter 3

When I was five, Mother and I moved to a boarding house in the University District of Minneapolis. This was to be the first of six such moves in the next seven and a half years. I remember arriving at a big, sprawling brick house. It had five wide brick steps leading to the front door. We entered into a huge foyer, went up a staircase to the second floor, and down to the end of a long hall. There was a small bedroom with two beds. This would be our home for the next two and a half years.

It was on a very busy street, and I was repeatedly cautioned never to cross that street alone. The streetcar stopped at the corner to take Mother downtown to her job every morning. She even worked a half-day on Saturday. The lady who ran the boarding house cared for me. Blanche soon came by to take me skating, but I wasn't allowed to go with her. I developed shooting pains in my legs each morning and screamed and clung to Mother as she tried to leave for work. But this did no good. Mother couldn't be late, or she would lose her job. The streetcar never left without her.

As I remember, the pains finally just went away, probably because they served no purpose for me. They did not bring back Mother and Blanche in the way I wanted them to. I also saw how badly they worried Mother. She looked terrified as she attempted to rub my legs to make the pain stop. I feared she would be so frightened that she wouldn't be able to be my mother anymore. In my mind, I had already lost Aunt Lida and the Portland family. I feared I was losing Blanche. Could I lose Mother too?

The boarding house was full of college students and young working people, mostly women. It contained an exciting energy. Mealtimes resounded with enthusiastic and mysterious chatter that I didn't understand but liked to listen to. One of the college girls gave me a brown toy dog named Toogee.

She had broken up with the boyfriend who had given it to her. Toogee joined Mary Marie in a central place in my life. They lived on my bed, and I slept with Mary Marie and Toogee every night.

I made up solitary ways to play. I tried to dress up in Mother's clothes and play imaginary games, pretending I was a lady, but Mother soon put a stop to that. I lined up all my toys against the wall in the hall and pretended they were a parade. I hosted tea parties with Mary Marie and Toogee using toy dishes. I colored and drew pictures and attempted to cut them out. I played with jigsaw puzzles, Tinker Toys, and building blocks.

The main problem was that I played in such a confined area, and naturally, I never picked anything up or put it away after I had played with it. Mother came home at the end of her day to what seemed to her a disaster area. She tried scolding me, but it had little result. Finally, she began setting the alarm clock for thirty minutes before she was due to come home. I was supposed to pick up my toys when the alarm went off. This did help some, although I was so engrossed in my play that the alarm frightened me when it went off. This remained an issue for us. Mother's life had changed so drastically from her life with you in Portland in your lovely, spacious, childless house.

One Saturday, we were in the backyard where Mother was hanging some clothes on the clothesline. She was holding clothespins in her mouth, and she was very angry with me. I can't remember what I had done, but she was furious. When she got mad like this, she would ignore me and refuse to speak to me. I couldn't stand this, and my terror was unbearable.

Finally, I remember crying out, "Do you love me?"

She took the clothespins out of her mouth and without looking at me, spat out, "No, not when you act like that."

I threw myself facedown on the grass, sobbing. I remember clawing at the grass with my fingers. Mother went into the house. Finally, exhausted from the fear and crying, I crept up to my bed and went to sleep. When I woke up, it was as if it had never happened. Mother was her normal self again.

How we needed you! You would have picked me up and befriended me while Mother dealt with her anger. Children need two parents, two alive and healthy parents, not a dead parent who is gone forever. Mothers need fathers, real flesh-and-blood fathers, to take over at times when they are at the end of their patience. Years later, when I had my own children, I understood that. But that was many years away.

Recently, I joined a class at church working with the spiritual healing of memories. As I prayed with this group of participants, I visualized myself back in that incident in search of my own healing from the trauma. As we prayed, Jesus appeared in that backyard. I lay sobbing, and he picked me up in his arms and sat down on a bench. I put my arms around him, put my head on his shoulder, and continued sobbing, my tears soaking his cloak.

Still in my prayer, Mother put down the clothespins and approached us. Holding me tightly, Jesus kissed the top of my head as he encompassed both of us in a gaze of love and understanding too deep to describe. As she met Jesus' gaze, I glimpsed an expression of sadness and longing mixed with tenderness and confusion on Mother's face—an expression that I saw very few times in our life together. I saw it in this prayer, twenty years after her death.

Mother had a Bible with an inscription indicating it had been given to her as a young teenager when she graduated from a Methodist Sunday school. One day, I saw her reading it, curled up on her bed like she was reading an ordinary book. Was she searching for where you might be? Was she searching for understanding and comfort?

One morning, she told me that she had dreamed she was going down in a glass elevator. She could see into the adjoining elevator, and as it went up, she could see you inside. But you were going up, and she was going down, and there was no way she could get to you.

When I was six, I asked Mother what it was like for you, shut away in your casket. Did she think you felt hot? Apparently, I was curious about your body. She told me never, never to talk that way again. So I didn't.

I began attending Sunday school at a Congregational Church a few blocks from where we lived. I remember being with other children in a classroom with a picture on the wall of Jesus blessing children. The teachers led us in a little worship service. Often, it was my turn to light the candles—carefully supervised, to be sure. We listened to Bible stories and sang songs while Miss West, one of the teachers, played the piano. I remember "Jesus Loves Me" and "Jesus Loves the Little Children". Sometimes we sang "Onward Christian Soldiers" as we marched around the room. (This was probably on the days we were especially restless, and the teachers thought marching might help.)

On Mother's Day, we dressed as flowers and went into the big church. We went down the aisle to the very front and formed a Mother's Day bouquet. I was a sweet pea. Each year, we had a Sunday called Children's Day where the children sang songs and recited poems during the service. Since I memorized so quickly, I always got to say a long poem. I loved it.

After Sunday school, I sat with Mother in the church service. I wore a short little dress, and the cushions on the pews were scratchy to my legs, so Mother spread out her handkerchief for me to sit on. I sat so proudly beside her, my legs dangling and my bottom squarely in the middle of the handkerchief. Church was long, but somehow I didn't mind.

Reverend Gregory, the pastor, always greeted Mother and me personally as we left the church. His wife, Mrs. Gregory, was one of my Sunday school teachers. As we walked out the door hand in hand, other people smiled and told Mother what a smart and lovely child I was. She beamed. It was truly a church home.

I started kindergarten several months after we moved to this first boarding house. Mother took time off work to go with me on that first day.

"Her father has died," I heard Mother say to the lady registering me. She had left a line blank on the form she was given to fill out. Mother's words were quick and her voice was strained. She sounded quite different, like her throat was closing up, and she had to get the words out quickly before it did. The woman said "Oh" in a soft voice, lengthening the word as she spoke it. Her face looked sad, and she quickly looked back down at the form. I felt like I was different from everyone else in a peculiar way I didn't understand.

The next day, Mother put a picture of you in our room. I had never seen what you looked like before. Years later, she told me she got out the picture because she was afraid people would think I was illegitimate.

How I wish you had been with us when I started school. I imagine us in our Portland home. You would have delighted in me, enjoying this special day. You would have given me a hug and kiss and told me what a big girl I was and how pretty I looked. I would twirl around in front of you, and you would admire my new dress and my special hair ribbon. Then you would go to work.

Mother and I would walk to school. Mother would look over all the mothers and children and make sure I would associate with the ones that met her approval. Registration quickly completed, I would run ahead of her into the classroom. She would walk home, realizing that now, at last, she could look forward to more order in her day. She might secretly be proud of me and of herself for coming this far. In the evening, I would sit on your lap and tell you all about my first day at school.

But this is the fantasy of a child. As I reflect on it now, I must remember that this was still the Depression, and your business was slow even before you became ill. We might have become poor. Mother may have had to go to work, but we would all still have each other.

I loved school. I loved being with the other children; I loved the stories, painting, and drawing, and I loved having my pictures put up on the wall. I loved recess, games, and singing. I remember being scolded for talking out of turn and interrupting and for not sitting still during story time. However, by first grade, I had learned the rules, and my deportment had apparently settled down.

Years later, I discovered a very early report card in a trunk. It described me as having a "rather excitable temperament" but with "a power to control situations." I was myself a mother when I read this, and my rather excitable temperament was close to the surface, but I was glad to have the power to at least sometimes control situations.

It was soon discovered that I was left-handed. My first-grade teacher took me aside and asked me to perform special activities, like catching and throwing a ball and copying shapes on a piece of paper. This was to determine which hand I was supposed to use. I loved the attention that I got from this and am grateful that no one ever tried to change this left-handedness. They were very good teachers. Three of my four sons are left-handed as well as one of my grandsons.

At Christmas, we made gifts for our parents. My teacher always asked me who I would give my father gift to. I always gave it to Freddy. When I was in kindergarten, I made him a tie rack. It hung in his closet for years. But I grieve so deeply because it was really yours.

In January of first grade, I got sick with a bad cold that turned into a sinus infection with a chronic fever. This meant staying home in bed in our small room for five weeks, missing school, Sunday school, and all the friends, learning, and activities that meant so much to me. Mary Marie and Toogee were my companions. Mother got me settled and gave me breakfast and my medicine before she left for work. The lady who ran the boarding house brought me lunch. When Mother came home after work, she brought me my dinner, read me stories, and cared for me.

One evening, Reverend Gregory came to see me, coming up the stairs and down the hall to our room. I remember the flurry of activity that surrounded this. Someone alerted Mother that Reverend Gregory was coming up the stairs. She jumped up, managed to put out her cigarette, put the ash tray under the bed, straightened the room with one fell swoop, whisked me into a clean pajama top, brushed the crumbs off my bed, combed her hair, and met him at the door in what could not have been longer than thirty seconds.

He brought me a gift. Had Mrs. Gregory been behind this? When I opened it, I found a box of valentines for me to cut out and send to my friends.

The illness went on so long that finally Mother arranged for a college girl to come in the afternoon to be with me. One day, she was settling me down for a nap, and she tried to take Mary Marie and Toogee out of the bed. Of course, I hung on to Mary Marie, clutching her in both arms and protesting at the top of my lungs.

The conflict escalated. She took hold of Mary Marie's head, which was the only grip available to her by then. I hung on, and she pulled. Mary Marie's head came off in her hands. When Mother came home, I was still sobbing as the college girl looked on helplessly. Mother sighed and put Mary Marie and her head in a paper sack, and she put the sack on the closet shelf.

When Mother turned her back, I jumped out of bed, ran down the hall, down the stairs, and out the front door. In my bare feet, I ran all the way around the block in my pajamas. It was Minneapolis in January. It was already dark, but I knew I could run forever. I still remember the ecstasy I felt as I breathed the freezing air while moving my body full speed to its very limits. I swung my arms in rhythm with my strong legs as I whizzed by snow-covered yards with icicles hanging from bare branches.

As I rounded the last corner, there was Mother in the front yard, desperately looking up and down the street. I was put to bed with my feet wrapped in a flannel blanket and two extra blankets on the bed. I was given an extra dose of medicine for good measure and no dinner and no story. I received the silent treatment from Mother for a day or so, and the college girl quit the job. It was just Toogee and me now. I spent the next day cutting out my valentines.

I finally got well, and we went to Blanche and Freddy's house for Sunday dinner. Blanche inquired about Mary Marie, noting that she had not come with us. She managed to extract the story, carefully interviewing both Mother and me.

"Mary Marie can be fixed," she insisted. "We will take her to the doll hospital."

I have never heard of a doll hospital since that time, but I can say that they had them in Minneapolis in 1939. The next Saturday, Blanche came to pick me up and retrieved Mary Marie from the closet shelf. We took Mary Marie downtown, still in her sack. I refused to hold the sack because it made me feel too sad. By that time, I wanted its grotesque contents to stay hidden away forever. I remember Blanche sitting beside me on the streetcar, holding the sack squarely on her lap. We went to the first doll hospital.

The man behind the counter looked in the sack, and then, still looking, put his hand inside and felt its contents. Perhaps he didn't want to expose the doll when he saw the look of anguish on my small face.

"This doll cannot be fixed," he proclaimed, shaking the sack a bit as if to bring emphasis to his words. I knew it. I pressed close to Blanche to keep my body from shaking.

"Then we will go somewhere else," Blanche said, putting her purse over her arm and picking up the sack. Then she took my hand, and we marched out of the shop.

We walked to the second doll hospital. The man behind the counter also looked in the sack and then looked at me, right into my upturned eyes. My chin and fingers were resting on the top of his counter. I was trying to be a big girl and not cling to Blanche. Clinging to the counter seemed to give some sense of stability. I watched as he took both parts of Mary Marie out of the sack and held the body in one hand and the head in the other, and moving his hands, carefully fitted both parts of the doll together. I noticed that Mary Marie was wearing her blue dress but only had one blue bootie. He held the doll like that for a while, carefully looking at her. Finally, he looked at Blanche and nodded his head.

"Yes, yes; it can be fixed," he said. I can still remember those words.

"We will need to leave her there a long time," Blanche cautioned as we left the shop. Looking back, as I skipped out the door, I saw the man still holding Mary Marie together, and he seemed to be thinking.

It did take a long time. Whenever we went to her house for dinner, I asked Blanche about the doll. Each time she assured me that Mary Marie was being fixed, and it just took time. I needed to learn to be patient.

After a very long time, it was Christmas, and we went to Blanche and Freddy's for Christmas Eve dinner and opening presents. There was a big present under the tree that I knew was for me. Dinner went on forever. I had to eat six green beans along with a piece of ham, two bites of potatoes, and a spoonful of Jell-O salad.

Finally, I could open my present. I ripped and ripped the long strands of cumbersome tissue paper, and I saw a doll high chair with Mary Marie sitting in it. She was whole and smiling at me as if she had never been broken. Hung over the high chair were new doll clothes for her—once again, all of them were handmade by Blanche.

Blanche, Freddy, and Mother sat by the tree sipping their coffee and watching me holding Mary Marie. I wouldn't entrust her to the new high chair yet. She only seemed safe in my arms. Mary, Joseph, the Christ child, the animals, and angels were in their traditional places on the living room table. Were they blessing us? You should have been there. But were you there? Were you in the hands and heart of the man who finally fixed Mary Marie? Were you sending us a blessing as well?

Chapter 4

When I was almost seven, Mother and I went back to Portland for a visit.

I was well traveled by then because we had taken the train back and forth several times before we settled in Minneapolis. Mother enjoyed the trips, perhaps because they were reminiscent of her time working for the railroads. She enjoyed the leisure and the attentive porters who waited on her every wish. There were few children on the train, so I frequently received notice and attention. Other passengers told her that I was adorable, and she beamed. I had Mother's undivided attention for two days. She read books over and over to me. I colored in my coloring book, and she admired my work. She praised me when I didn't drop any crayons under our seats. I quickly learned to be very careful.

When the train stopped at a station, we went outside, and Mother told me to run as fast as I could up and down the platform. She smiled as she watched me run. I often went up and down six or seven times if it was a long stop. When the conductor blew the whistle, we got back on the train quickly. I was out of breath, a lot of my pent-up energy gone from my active little body. Usually, I was ready for a nap.

In the dining car, Mother told me I could have anything I wanted to eat. I couldn't read menus so she may have edited the choices before she presented them. The food was elegant, and Mother savored her meals. There were no green beans, and I loved the mashed potatoes. I had ice cream for dessert every night.

Of course, Mary Marie was with us, and at night, she slept in a small net hammock strung under the window in our sleeping berth. Mother said the hammock was really a place for her to put her purse. But it became Mary Marie's bed, and I dressed her in her pajamas and tucked her there with her doll blanket snuggly around her. The rhythmic sound and movement of the train lulled all three of us to sleep. Train trips were oases in our life.

When we got to Portland, there was the feeling of not knowing anyone who seemed to know me. I remember going to Portland Memorial Mausoleum, where, in mysterious tones, I was told my daddy was buried. Mother and Aunt Lida carried flowers and acted strangely.

I took off running. I ran up and down a long hall. I wouldn't stop running, so Uncle Earl got hold of me and took me out to the car. I cried, screamed, and carried on as we waited in the car. Uncle Earl told me I was being a brat. I didn't know what a brat was, but it felt good at that moment. It also felt good to get on the train for the journey back to Minneapolis.

We moved to another boarding house when I was halfway through second grade, and I changed schools. This new classroom was different and strange. I remember being scolded for not following directions, "daydreaming," or not finishing my work. But I remember the joy of finding out that I could read. There was a shelf of library books in one corner. I would lose myself in my reading and forget where I was to be or what I was supposed to do. I also found out that I could spell some words, and I could begin to write down my own ideas and experiences. This was the opening of a new and freeing world, one that I could quietly explore with total abandon.

Soon after we moved, Uncle Raymond, Aunt Gertrude, and their two children came from Portland to visit us. This was a very special event. Mother prepared for it for days, and how glad she was to see them! They were eager to get to know me, see how we lived, and find out what I was like, now that I was old enough to be in school. I saw how very special we were to them. It was the first time I had been close to a family of two parents with their children. I watched Uncle Raymond help care for his son and daughter, and I longed for him to care for me as well. But I knew I was different. I desperately felt a hole in my own life. Was I missing something necessary, something that only I knew about? It frightened me.

We moved again at the end of the school year, and I started third grade in a different school.

It wasn't a real boarding house this time. We lived in a regular house with a mother and a nine-year-old daughter—a year older than I—and a father who was there for a while. The daughter, Gail, had a room of her own, but I shared Mother's room. This was in a new, upscale suburb of Minneapolis, which Mother really appreciated.

I loved that there were kids on the block to play with. We jumped rope and roller-skated up and down the sidewalk. I got a bike for my birthday and struggled to finally learn to ride it. On summer evenings, we played "kick the can" until it was almost dark. In the winter, neighborhood girls came over to play, or sometimes we played at their houses. Mother encouraged this, telling me those were just the right people to associate with. These girls had fathers who came home for dinner at 5:00, and we had to stop our playing and go home. In the summer, the fathers mowed the lawns on Saturday and took their families swimming at a nearby lake on Sunday afternoon. I observed these fathers with intense interest and thought they were remarkable creatures.

We had a play space in the basement where we kept all of our toys and games. Gail and I played there, and that's where we played when friends came over. But sometimes, when no one else was around, I went down there and discovered that I was afraid to be alone in that place. I feared that you might appear to me as a ghost. I longed for you to come back, be home at 5:00 for dinner, mow the lawn, and take me swimming. But would you appear as a ghost? When this fear came over me, I ran quickly back up the stairs.

When there was no one to play with, I would stay upstairs and read books. I brought as many books home from the school library as I was allowed at one time, and Mother and Blanche would buy me books for birthdays and Christmas. I read beyond my grade level and often beyond my ability. If I didn't know a word, I would skip it and get the idea of the story as best I could without it. Sometimes I didn't know a great number of the words, but I got enough of the story to keep me going.

I ran into trouble of a different kind when I read *Bambi*. Bambi is a young deer whose mother is shot and killed by hunters. I couldn't bear it as I read this. I was terrified that this could be allowed to happen—in a book or anywhere. Mother tried to comfort me, telling me it was just a story that was not really true. But that didn't take away my terror.

I heard Mother tell Gail's mother that I was "high-strung." I didn't know what "high-strung" meant and feared it meant I was going insane. Later, *Bambi* became a movie. I was never able to read the book or see the movie with my own children, or even to this day, with my grandchildren.

Each evening, Mother continued a ritual that went on for way too many more years. She would put me in the bathtub and give me a bath, washing and examining every part of my growing body with an earnest, determined look on her face that never wavered. Sometimes I would attempt to get the washcloth and soap away from her and wash myself. I would tell her to go away and leave alone. But she always hung on, scolding me that I was splashing water on the floor. I would argue with her, but it did no good. When I pointed out that Gail and everyone else I knew bathed themselves, she said that I was not as capable as they were and added that this was not my house and I couldn't splash water on the floor, or I might get sick or cold if I stayed in the bathroom or the bathtub by myself.

Usually, I just spaced out as this bathing was occurring, moving obediently to every position she required and accepting it as inevitable. I needed you to put a stop to this, to allow me to have control and confidence in my growing body. It was the only way I had Mother's touch and undivided attention. When I stayed all night with Blanche, I took my own bath in the bathroom alone, and it was wonderful. I had lots of Blanche and Freddy's undivided attention as well.

In the family where we lived, the father was hardly there. After a while, he moved out, and we learned he had a girlfriend. Gail cried for hours. I could hear wailing and sobbing in her room where the door was shut. At last, she came out, still sobbing with her eyes red and her face pale and swollen. She had decided to run away, and she asked me to go with her. I wanted to go so badly but knew I couldn't leave my mother. Mother would never forgive me, and I would have nowhere to go. So I walked with Gail to the corner and watched her take off on her bicycle. I told no one. When I went to bed that night, I was awake for hours. Finally, very late, I heard doors slamming and loud voices scolding. Apparently, someone had found her and brought her home. I went to sleep, and nothing more was said about this in the morning.

School was different that year. For one thing, I rode a school bus, which was a strange, new experience. I also got in trouble in class quite a bit. The work was boring, and I daydreamed when I was supposed to be working. I was scolded nearly every day for talking out of turn, getting out of my seat without permission, not finishing my work, and—a big one—disturbing my neighbor. My neighbor usually didn't mind being disturbed, but I was the one who was scolded

I lived for recess when the girls jumped long rope on the playground. Two girls held each end of a long piece of clothesline and turned the rope so the others could jump into it. We took turns running in and jumping the rope, one or two of us at a time. When you stumbled and missed, it was your turn to hold an end of the rope. There was one really nice teacher who would sometimes turn one end for us for the entire recess. As we jumped, we chanted rhymes and acted out the gestures. Here is one I remember:

Teddy Bear, Teddy Bear, turn around.
Teddy Bear, Teddy Bear, touch the ground.
Teddy Bear, Teddy Bear, show your new shoes.
Teddy Bear, Teddy Bear, read the news.
Teddy Bear, Teddy Bear, run up the stairs.
Teddy Bear, Teddy Bear, say your prayers.
Teddy Bear, Teddy Bear, turn out the light.
Teddy Bear, Teddy Bear, say good night.

If we made it all the way through without missing, we said "good night" very loudly as we successfully jumped out of the rope. I was very good at this, even not missing the part where you had to touch the ground while jumping. I wish you had been there to watch me.

I joined a Brownie troop along with other girls who were my friends from school. One of the mothers was our leader, and we met after school at her home. We learned about the importance of doing good deeds for people. We baked cookies and made cards to give to people in the hospital. We sang songs at a nursing home. We also played games and went on outings to the park where we ate delicious snacks. I loved being with the other girls, and I appreciated the loving attention all of us received from this mother.

Another change was eating lunch at school. Before, I had always gone home for lunch. Now, we all bought a hot lunch, which tasted terrible. We went through a cafeteria line, got food, and carried our trays to long tables to eat. We were not allowed to talk as we ate our lunch. One day, I couldn't get my chair underneath the table, so I forgot about not talking and asked the girl next to me to move her chair. A teacher swooped down on me.

"Janet," she said—and her voice could be heard the length of the room. "Bring your tray and come with me." I picked up my tray and followed her out of the room while all the silent lunch-eaters watched in trepidation. Managing not to spill my food, I followed her down a long hall into the furnace room.

The janitor was sitting at a table eating his lunch. "Janet will need to eat her lunch here with you," the teacher commanded. I stood, holding my tray, paralyzed with terror. The janitor stood up, gave me a kindly look, and took my tray from me. Gesturing to the teacher to go back to the lunchroom, he set my tray on the table across from his, pulled out my chair, and gestured to me to sit down as if I were an important lady. My tears started to flow.

He began visiting with me as he ate his lunch, not expecting a response, but continuing a friendly conversation. He pretended not to notice that I wasn't eating, and he made no mention of my tears. I began to relax. When he had finished eating, he politely asked me if I was finished. I nodded, and he said for me to run along out to the playground, and he would return my tray to the lunchroom. He held the door open for me and smiled. I looked back, and he was still smiling an encouraging smile as I made my way back up the hall. I wonder if he was an angel sent from you to protect me.

One Sunday morning, I heard Mother on the stair landing talking on the phone. "Oh, no; oh, no," she kept repeating anxiously. Running to her, I watched her troubled face as she sat on the bottom step and spoke again into the phone. "Oh, no; oh, no; oh, no," she said, slowly shaking her head. The Japanese had bombed Pearl Harbor in Honolulu, and Blanche was phoning with the news. "We're at war," Mother exclaimed when at last she hung up the phone.

"Will it come here?" I searched her face for an answer. Hawaii was half a continent and an ocean away, but in my mind, I pictured it down the street.

"They won't get this far," Mother reassured me.

But before long, we had blackout drills. All the lights had to be out all over the city. If an airplane with a bomb should fly over us, it would go away because it didn't know where to drop the bomb.

Freddy was an air raid warden in his neighborhood. He walked around outside during a drill, making sure all the homes had their lights out. He had a bucket of sand and first aid equipment with him to help in case there was ever a real bomb. I asked him how he could see in the dark.

"Air raid wardens are the only people who can have flashlights on," he explained. "But if a plane should fly over, they are supposed to turn them off."

Children in my class had fathers fighting in the war, but I think I was just as anxious about Freddy being outside in a blackout drill. Years later, after I grew up, I was in a gathering of people reminiscing about that war. One of the women had been in London during the German bombing and another had been in the Philippines during the Japanese occupation. I realized that I carried more fearful memories of that time than these women, who had been little girls in immediate physical danger.

We had air raid drills at school. When a siren went off, we walked to the coatroom, picked up our coats, went out in the hall, and crouched against the wall with our coats over our heads. The teachers walked up and down the hall to make sure our heads were under our coats. I knew that if it were a real bomb, the teachers would be hit.

"Coat over your head, Janet." A teacher would go by and spot me popping up and looking around. I couldn't stand not to look, so I popped up again and again. After I did this a few times, a teacher would stand right by me to make sure my head was covered. At least she was nearby, and I could feel her presence, but I knew she could be taken away forever by a bomb.

We brought a dime to school every Friday, which was bank day. We purchased a stamp to lick and put in a special book. When the book was full, it was enough money to buy a war bond. I didn't know how this worked, but somehow the bond money went to help the soldiers and make the war end sooner.

People complained about the food and gas rationing. Everyone had ration books. Mother was outraged because she had to put her date of birth on her food ration book. She gave our books to whoever shopped for the groceries where we were living. Mother protested that everyone would know how old she was. Years later, I learned that she had written a date five years younger than her actual age.

A lady at work invited Mother to join a group of ladies who folded bandages for the Red Cross one evening a week. Mother told her that the Red Cross never did anything for her, and she was not about to do anything for them.

"I hate war," Mother muttered. "It makes my life even harder than it is already."

This was a marked contrast to what I was learning in school and in my Brownie troop about things we could do to help our soldiers win the war. Blanche was doing work for the Red Cross, and I felt good about that.

That summer after third grade, we moved again. I said good-bye to Gail, my playmates on the block, and my Brownie troop. We moved out of the suburbs and back to Minneapolis to another real boarding house.

This was a large house but with far fewer boarders. The house was managed by a lady who I will call Mrs. P. She had a teenaged daughter and another daughter who was grown up and working but still lived there. The boarders were two single middle-aged women, Mother, and I. There were no men in the house. We all ate dinner together at a big dining room table. Since I was supposed to be quiet and let the grown-ups talk, I learned quite a bit about the lives of grown-ups at dinner. The arrangement was as before; the lady was to care for me when Mother was at work.

I started fourth grade in a new school. It meant making new friends, but I liked school. The things we learned and the work we did were interesting. My behavior problems seemed to smooth out. I was getting older and was able to read, write, think, and absorb learning in ways that were exciting and challenging, and the girls jumped long rope at recess.

The school library was a treasure trove. I checked out books by the armful. *Lassie* became my dog. Laura Ingalls Wilder's family struggles on the frontier became my struggles. Kate Seredy's books, *The Good Master* and *The Singing Tree,* transported me into a girl's life growing up on a farm in Hungary. I wanted to live on the farm next door, go to school with her, and be her friend. I read every book Elizabeth Enright wrote as fast as it appeared on the shelf. I especially enjoyed *The Saturdays,* which was about what it was like being a child in a big, interesting family.

My greatest discovery was *Little Women* by Louisa Mae Alcott. I lost myself in this story of four sisters growing up in a family during the Civil War. They became my sisters; the parents became my parents and their family life, my life. Beth, one of the sisters, dies in the course of the book. In my imagination, I live the reality of the death through the lenses of this nurturing family. Even in their despair, they were brimming with faith and love for one another.

Between the ages of nine and twelve, I read this book more than twenty times. It was formative in my life, and I owe it a great deal. In my secret inner self, it opened the door of imagination to a way of understanding, a way of claiming and honoring our loss of one another and bearing the abortive fracture of our family. There were two sequels to the book that carried the girls into adulthood with their own marriages and families. Just as I still emulate Blanche in the many practical ways that I manage my outer life, I still notice these sisters in the landscape of my imaginative inner life.

There were school friends in the neighborhood to play with. Although they could not come into my house, I played at their houses. We rode our bicycles and roller-skated up and down the sidewalks. In the winter, a nearby vacant lot was made into an ice-skating rink. I got ice skates for Christmas from Mother, and, of course, I loved to skate. The Minneapolis winter was cold, but I twirled around the ice not feeling the slightest bit encumbered by a heavy wool snowsuit, wool hat, mittens, a large woolen muffler around my neck, and two pairs of wool socks under my skates. I could fly.

I joined a Brownie troop, which became a Girl Scout troop as soon as we were ten years old. One of the girl's mothers was our leader, and I remember her as being very pretty and full of energy and patience. She was always teaching us and praising our efforts as we tried something new. We each designed and embroidered a border on a cotton placemat. The placemats were to go to soldiers who had been wounded and were in the hospital. She sat by me at the table where we all worked and gave me extra help when I tangled my thread. The troop all went to Girl Scout camp the summer I was ten, but no matter how hard the leader tried to persuade her, Mother refused to let me go because she was afraid I might get appendicitis. Sometimes I woke in the night to Mother leaning over my bed, shaking me. She would say that she had a dream that I was smothering in my sleep.

The upstairs in the house where our room and bathroom were was very cold. Mrs. P. said it could not be warmer because of the fuel rationing. But the downstairs, where her room was located, was warmer, along with the rest of the house. I noticed the cold the mostly after school when I played or read in my room. She turned the heat up a bit when the working ladies came home. I piled on sweaters and sometimes put a blanket around me as well. Then I absorbed myself in my reading or in imaginative play with Mary Marie and Toogee, who now lived in a doll bed in the corner of our room.

Although I was nearly ten years old, Mother continued to insist on completely bathing me nightly. I protested, but she said she didn't want me to get sick. I felt helpless and humiliated. I knew other girls were not treated like this. It was Mother's and my secret, and I hated having it. I needed you to be there to make this stop.

When Mother was at work, Mrs. P. was crabby and critical. I ate my breakfast after Mother left for work. By then, there was a crust on the pot of oatmeal, and my dish always included a portion of this crust. I came home for lunch, and it was always leftover dinner from the night before. I longed for a peanut butter sandwich. I could have nothing between the meals as Ms. P. said it would give me diabetes. Sometimes Mother would bring home candy for both of us. When Mrs. P. saw me eating it, she started in about the diabetes again. There were no meals in the boarding house on Sunday evening, so Mother and I went to a restaurant. I lived for Sunday night and the wonderful food choices I had in the restaurant, which included a large dessert and Mother's undivided attention. Mother seemed to enjoy these times as well.

When I look back on pictures from this time, I notice how very thin I am. I was not eating enough food. I was growing very tall by then. Goodness, it must have taken Mother longer to bathe me each year.

I began to complain to Mother about the cold, the hunger, and the diabetes threats.

She said that it was my job to get along. If I didn't, we would be out in the street with no place to live, and it would be my fault. She then sighed and said that she thought I would grow up to be a help to her, but she guessed I never would. I stopped complaining.

After school, huddled in my sweaters and blanket, in my childlike imagination, you, Mother, and I all lived together in our Portland home with warm rooms and peanut butter sandwiches and desserts every day. We didn't fear war, sickness, death, or that there would be no place to live because we were together, safe in our love for each other. And I had a huge bathtub behind a closed door, all my own.

There was a piano in the living room, and I began to take piano lessons. Mother said that she had always wanted to play the piano, so she wanted me to learn this. She insisted that if you could play the piano you would always associate with the right people when you grew up. I asked if I could take dancing lessons instead, but this went nowhere. Piano lessons it was.

The good part was that the living room, where I was supposed to practice every day after school, was warm. Also, I finally learned once and for all to tell my right hand from my left hand by imagining myself at a piano facing the bass clef and treble clef. The bad part was that I hated to practice, and although I enjoyed pleasing Mother so much, I really didn't like the piano.

The piano teacher was patient with my often choppy lessons. If I had a good lesson, I got a sticker. If I got ten stickers, I got a statue of a famous composer. Somehow this appealed to me, and small busts of Beethoven, Bach, Paderwiski, and others began to adorn the top of our dresser. Mother loved it. She also loved the recitals. All the children were dressed up, and we played our pieces beginning with the youngest and ending with the oldest. The other parents told Mother what a beautiful and charming child I was and how well I played. These parents must have been the right people to associate with. After the recital, everyone went together to Bridgemen's ice cream parlor for big ice cream sodas. We stayed up very late.

The summer that I turned ten, Mother enrolled me in a two-week Vacation Bible School at a church two blocks away from where we lived. After we left the University District, we had stopped going to church and Sunday school. The Sunday school teachers at the Congregational Church drove over and picked me up at our new place for a while, but finally that faded away. I missed it, and the Vacation Bible School sounded like it could be fun. I did have some misgivings when it seemed like none of my friends in the neighborhood would be going. Mother said that was because they were all Catholic. I got the feeling that Catholics were not that magical "right people."

I liked my Catholic friends. They had large families, which often included a baby. They had to do chores before they could come outside. They sounded so capable. They had big yards and large front porches where there were always children eager to play. Their mothers were always home. They went to a special school and a special church, which to me sounded mysteriously inviting. I could tell this worried Mother.

The Vacation Bible School church was dark and plain and nothing like the quiet beauty I remembered from the Congregational Church. A metal tank, like a small swimming pool, was on a raised platform that almost took over the entire front of the church.

I was told you got all the way into this tank of water to be born again and baptized. But first, you needed to give your heart to Jesus. The pastor was not at all like Reverend Gregory. He sat on the edge of the platform, played the accordion, and led the singing.

When we weren't singing, he talked about the importance of being born again and giving your heart to Jesus. He said there was one way to Jesus. He held up a picture of Jesus knocking on a door with a latch that was on its other side. It was the door to open to be with Jesus. Jesus couldn't open it from his side. We sang a song that still makes me shudder as I remember it:

One door and only one and yet the sides are two.
Inside and outside on which side are you?
One door and only one and yet the sides are two.
I'm on the inside and which side are you?

When we sang the last line, we turned to one another and drew a question mark in the air with our fingers.

This gave me an anxiety that increased as we went through the first week and into the second week. In the classroom, we did art projects, read Bible stories, and played games, but the teachers didn't give me the loving attention that I remembered receiving at Sunday school. This made me mad, and I asked Mother if I could quit attending. She said it was all paid for, and I had to finish that second week.

One morning, I got there early and was the first one in the classroom. The teacher sat down beside me and asked if I was born again and had given my heart to Jesus. I had the presence of mind to tell her that I knew I had been baptized even though not in a tank. She said that was not enough. She asked me to kneel down on the floor with her, open the door, and give my heart to Jesus.

I was trapped. I was afraid another child would come into the room and see us. We knelt down, and she prayed something. Then she told me to give my heart to Jesus in my own words. I wanted this to be over, so I told Jesus I would give him my heart. We got up, and she said she was very proud of me. The other children joined us, and the day began.

Jesus seemed close to me. Not the loving Jesus I thought I knew before, but a disapproving Jesus. It seemed like Jesus disapproved of me for believing many of the things my mother said and did, most particularly bathing me. To be right with Jesus, I had to stop this even if it meant destroying my mother. I felt sick, alone, and ashamed. I needed her so badly, and I knew in my heart she would not change.

Finally, the morning was over, and I ran for home. Mrs. P. wasn't there, and the door was locked. I sat outside on the steps needing to go to the bathroom. This was really what it was like to be outside the door.

At last Mrs. P. came home. I was sick the rest of the day. I had to choose between Jesus and Mother, and I was falling apart from grief. That night, when Mother was bathing me, I sat straight up in the tub, grabbed the washcloth, and told her what happened that day. I was so upset that she paused and listened to me.

I remember a troubled look on her face. She told me not to worry, that this was a strange church and Jesus loved all children. She continued with the bathing. I had so many questions. I wanted someone to really talk to. The most important question was did Jesus love all grown-ups too? Perhaps this church wasn't strange. Maybe we were strange. Perhaps Jesus didn't love either of us, and I was supposed to do something about it. Mother said I didn't have to finish out the second week of Bible school. I was sick anyway and stayed in bed reading my familiar library books.

A month after Bible school, Mother and I went on a two-week vacation to a resort on a lake in Northern Minnesota. It was an oasis in our lives, like the earlier train rides. Mother was happy, soaking up the leisure, enjoying the wonderful food and all the right people to associate with. There was a golf course, and she accepted invitations to play golf. I remember being told that you and she played golf during your marriage. Perhaps this is what our life together would have been like if you had not died.

There were many families with children, and we all played together, usually swimming and enjoying the beach. The other parents seemed to like us. They wanted to include Mother in their social times, and they wanted me to play with their children. At bedtime, when Mother was still sitting on a porch visiting with people, I made a beeline for our bathroom and took my bath.

One afternoon, Mother and I took a walk along the lake to a store that sold baskets. She bought me a small basket to take home. It was where I kept my trinkets. Years and years later, when she died and I went through her things, I found the basket in her cedar chest. It was one of the few things that she kept forever, long after I grew up. As we got on the bus that was to take us home, I couldn't keep back tears. Mother laughed and didn't seem to know how to respond to my tears. I wonder if she had secret tears sometimes over the years when she looked at that basket.

"Ever since you and your mother got home, you have been impossible to live with," Mrs. P. lashed out. I must have been resisting her scolding, probably with a belligerent attitude. This was a surprising contrast to my former passive ways. I was sad because Mother had reverted to her old self as soon as the vacation was over.

Chapter 5

We moved soon after that. As I think back, it was a surprisingly different sort of place than Mother had chosen previously. We were not boarders; we shared a house with another single lady and her two boys. One of the boys was my age and the other was much younger. Supposedly, a housekeeper cared for us while the mothers went to work. However, we roamed free.

We had play space in the garage for our toys, games, and projects. We wrote plays and invited neighbor children to be actors and actresses. We could go anywhere without permission. We fixed our own lunches and had an unlimited choice of sandwich makings, store-bought cookies, and chocolate milk. I look back on the pictures from that time, and it looks like I gained some weight.

Many of the mothers on the block worked in the war plants, and their children were as unsupervised as were we. Next door, a very old grandmother was responsible for the children. One of the girls would hold the grandmother against the wall and bend her hand as if to break it to get her own way. The grandmother's eyes were terror-stricken. I saw this happen several times, and it horrified me, but there was no one to tell.

The boy that I lived with told me he wanted me to be his girlfriend, and he wanted to kiss me. I didn't want him to be this way, and it frightened me. What frightened me the most was the strange new feeling this evoked. There was a part of me that wanted him to kiss me. I needed a father, I needed parents, and I needed a family. I needed solid grown-ups with whom I could belong. Blanche was very perceptive.

"Janet, do you have a boyfriend?"

During Sunday dinner at her house, she took me aside and asked. I turned away, afraid to tell her what was going on. It was too soon to have a boyfriend, but I was both attracted and frightened by these intense feelings. She dropped the subject.

As much as I had hated Mrs. P. and had wanted to move, I was surprised at how much I missed my former school. I had left midyear, in fifth grade. We were beginning to study history and geography, and there were fascinating maps rolled up on the wall that the teacher pulled down dramatically each time she began a lesson.

She seated the class by our behavior and how accurately we did our work. She explained that the best seats were in the row closest to the maps, and I knew that the best seats in each row were the ones way in back. The students in those seats could be trusted to be that far away from the teacher's desk. For me, the strategy was to be close to the maps and as far as possible from the teacher's desk.

Each week, she evaluated her seating chart, and we could be moved up, down, or stayed in the same seat. I had just been moved to the back seat in the row nearest the maps.

In the new school, which I entered midterm, I was confused, bored, and sad, and I often felt unnoticed by the teacher. I also missed the skating rink, my Girl Scout troop, and my friends from the former neighborhood. I was freed from the piano lessons, but I missed the attention and celebration of the recitals.

We didn't live in that place very long. Before the sixth grade, we moved to another boarding arrangement back in the suburb where we had lived when I was in third grade. We lived with a family, Mr. and Mrs. H., a mother and father, and Ruby, a little girl five years younger than I.

It soon became apparent, even to me, that Mr. H. had a problem with alcohol. Often he would drink until he passed out. His wife helped him up the stairs to bed, and he slept well into the next day. Then this pattern would start all over again in a day or so. Mrs. H. must have been stressed to her limit, and I was the one who bothered her the most. She and Mother became friends, and Mother provided her with companionship and sympathy.

"I don't keep you here because I like you," she blurted out in one of her mad times. "I only keep you here because I love your mother."

Mother seemed charmed by Ruby. I was jealous, unwilling to share her limited attention and approval. I had no assurance of any privacy because that child could be anywhere. Although I was eleven years old, Mother continued the bathing ritual. Ruby knocked on the bathroom door. She kept knocking and finally Mother let her in.

"We have to let her in because this is her house," Mother would insist as I protested.

Ruby sat on the toilet seat, taking in my naked self being bathed by my mother.

"Get her out of here!" I shouted at Mother.

But it did no good. Mother seemed to see both of us as the same age. She wanted to keep me a little child like Ruby. She ignored the reality in front of her in the bathtub, that I was indeed growing up.

Mrs. H. enjoyed sewing and sewed beautifully. At Christmas, Mother and Mrs. H. had bought identical dolls for Ruby and me and made identical wardrobes of clothes for each doll. I was too old to be getting dolls for Christmas. I had never seen Mother sew like that before. She was mothering me the same way Mrs. H. mothered Ruby. I still treasured Mary Marie, but she was secretly tucked away in a drawer by this time. For Christmas, I asked for a special pleated skirt with matching sweater that was all the fashion at school. Mother said I wasn't old enough for such clothes.

There were many children to play with up and down the street. On summer evenings, we played "kick the can." The sounds of our running, laughing, and shouting could be heard all over the neighborhood. Then, as darkness settled in, there were the soothing sounds of parents calling their children to come in. We had wonderful birthday parties with presents, games, delicious food, and cake. On my birthday, Mother waited until Saturday and took a group of us girls to the ice cream parlor. These children in this affluent neighborhood were her kind of people.

In the spring and summer, we rode bicycles all around the neighborhood. The girls stopped to play in one another's houses. No one could play at my house, and we all seemed to take this for granted.

One fall day, we all came home from school, and there was no one at home yet in the house next door. The girl who was my age ran to our back door and asked if she could use the bathroom. Mrs. H. said she could not. So she went behind a bush, wet her pants, and took them off. Calmly, she went to her own clothesline where the weekly washing was hanging. She took a pair of dry, clean pants off the line, put them on, and carefully hung the wet ones in their place. I watched in amazement, impressed with how easily she made the best of the crisis. I was grateful that she didn't blame me after this glimpse of the way I lived. Her mother soon came home, and we all laughed together at the wet pants on the clothesline. She and I remained good friends.

Winters were snowy and cold in Minneapolis, and our outdoor play reflected this. In the winter, we went sledding on a hill in a nearby park. We also made forts out of the packed snow and then had snowball fights between the forts. When there was a fresh snowfall, we would lie down in the snow and move our arms and legs to make snow angels. The skill was in getting up without damaging the angel. Perfect angels were much admired.

Most of the families in the neighborhood were Jewish. Mother and Mrs. H. stressed that these were not our kind of people. But these Jewish mothers were lovely. They had maids to help with the housework, and they spent long summer days simply being with their children. They included me when they took everyone to the nearby lake for swimming and picnic lunches. The mothers told me how pretty I was and how beautiful I would be when I grew up.

"You will certainly be a movie star," one of them exclaimed. I basked in their attention. I was a red-haired, blued-eyed creature amidst a sea of Mediterranean loveliness, but was allowed to be beautiful and was appreciated and nurtured in ways I will never forget. Sometimes on Friday evenings, I stood at our dining room window and watched the Sabbath candles being lit with the family around the table in the dining room next door. I longed to be Jewish.

Back in this Minneapolis suburb, school was full of anxiety and stress. I began each day with a long ride on the school bus. Because of the war, the country was on double daylight saving time the year around. Therefore, 8:00 was really 6:00 by sun time. It was cold and dark waiting for the bus and dark for a long time after we got to school.

Although I had a warm jacket and ski pants, Mother made me wear two sets of underwear because she was afraid I would get sick. We changed into gym clothes for P.E. and took showers afterward. I couldn't hide my extra pair of underwear. I was teased somewhat, but, as I think back, this must have seemed so bizarre to the other girls that it went beyond something to tease.

My sixth-grade teacher yelled at the class. She had bad headaches and sometimes put her head down on the desk and just stayed there while we tried to do our work. I often felt like I didn't understand what we were supposed to do. She said some of us would not pass at the end of the year. I was in terror that I would have to repeat sixth grade. When report cards were distributed the last day of school, I was paralyzed at the thought of opening mine. But I did pass. One boy in the class did not pass, and he sat at his desk and wept. He was a wonderful boy, so good at sports, but he struggled with school. I have thought of him over the years and wondered how life turned out for him.

Seventh grade was better. Of course, I still had P.E., the showers, and the embarrassing double underwear, but we changed classes for some of the subjects, and the teachers were nicer. We took home economics, and I learned to read recipes and cook. I learned how to put together colors that match to furnish a house. We also learned to sew, and each girl made a white apron.

A note was sent home that we were to bring white cotton fabric to school to make the aprons. Mother wouldn't buy the fabric. She said she resented having to buy things for school and that I would just ruin it if she bought it. I was desperate because I had to have the fabric by a certain date. Finally, Mrs. H. gave me an old white crib sheet. "It has already been wet on," she remarked. "It doesn't matter if you ruin it." So my cotton was not fresh and new like the other girls. It caused a problem for the teacher because the size wasn't the same, and I needed more individual help. But I was so proud of the apron I made.

I went with my class on a field trip to the Minneapolis Repertory Theater to see a professional production of *Peter Pan*. I was instantly stage-struck. Sitting on the edge of my seat, I became the character of Wendy, enchanted by Peter and flying off to Never Never Land to be a mother to little boys who never grew up. The actors flew through the air, held by wires suspended over the stage. My heart flew with them. Oh, to be cherished and needed, to have a friend like Peter, to make a difference in such a rich, exciting, magical world. Oh, to be able to fly there. I have seen the play several more times over the years, and I still weep in the last scene as Wendy tells Peter she can no longer live in Never Never land. She must stay home and grow up. Peter tells her he will never grow up, and he is going back. He asks her to promise to come back just once a year to do their spring cleaning. Wendy agrees, and from my seat, I nod with her as I weep. There is still a little part of me that believes that life can be kept safe and unchanged by the powerful ritual of spring cleaning.

Mr. H. continued to drink heavily. One evening, he tumbled all the way down the stairs, landing flat on his back in the front hallway. He lay there several hours until he finally woke up and dragged himself back up the stairs.

One evening, Mother wasn't home. This was a rare occurrence, and he and Mrs. H. had a huge argument. I think that Mother's usual presence kept an argument of this magnitude from happening. He drank more and more as the evening and the argument went on. Mustering up my courage, I went up to him and cried out, "My dad may be dead, but he isn't drunk."

There was silence in the room. I thought I was gone for good. Then he started to sob. "I know; I know," he said over and over as he wept.

One evening, he got out his hunting rifle and said he was going to shoot himself. Mother, Ruby, and I ran upstairs, and Mrs. H. stayed with him trying to calm him down. Finally, she too came upstairs. He was stomping around, still ranting loudly that he would shoot himself. Mother told me to get ready for bed.

As I took off my clothes, I discovered I had gotten my period for the first time. I went to the top of the stairs, told Mother, and asked her for some Kotex. She didn't have any, so she asked Mrs. H. if she had any. Mrs. H. was leaning over the banister trying to talk to her husband, but she ran quickly, found what I needed, and resumed her stance leaning over the banister. Mother rolled her eyes. "This is about the last straw for the evening" she exclaimed.

Mr. H. finally put down the rifle, threw up on the rug, and passed out on the living room couch. We went to bed. The next morning, Mother said I didn't have to go to school. She put me in a taxi and sent me to spend the day at Blanche's house while she went to work.

Blanche greeted me at the door with a big smile. "You are becoming a young lady," she exclaimed. She fed me cinnamon toast and two cups of hot chocolate. She poured herself a cup of coffee, sat down, and we talked all morning. "When you grow up, be sure to have children," she said fervently.

"I know about these things," I bragged. "I learned about them in my health class at school."

"Don't listen to your mother," she warned me. "Listen to your health teacher. The reason I don't have children is because I was afraid. My mother told us that when you have a baby, you lie in a pool of blood."

I could see that this went along with Mother's fear of "living in squalor." Their other sister, Rene, never had children either. Blanche went on thoughtfully.

"Lucille was the only one of us to have a child, and that was not her wish. In fact, it was her greatest fear—she hated the very thought of it."

Blanche looked down and became quiet, seemingly absorbed in her own thoughts. I sipped my cocoa, careful not to disturb her reverie. At last, she looked up.

"I'm so glad you came along anyway," she announced.

She looked at me with her broad, familiar smile, and there was a twinkle in her eye as she got up to refill my cocoa cup.

When I grew all the way up, I was glad that I listened to my health teacher. I gave birth to four children. They are all boys—your grandsons. I never spent time in the land of lost boys who didn't grow up. But I still do spring cleaning and having these sons has been the greatest joy of my life. But I am way ahead of my story.

After lunch, I sat in the comfy chair in the living room and read *Gone with the Wind*, relishing my day off from school. I didn't tell Blanche about Mr. H.'s episode the night before. I never talked of these things to anyone. But becoming a young lady seemed exciting and full of possibilities.

But two months later, Blanche had a hysterectomy. She was in the hospital for two weeks. When she got home, it was my spring vacation from school, so Mother sent me over to be with her during the day while Freddy was at work. My job was to run errands, fix her lunch, and keep her company. But she spent most of the day lying on the couch, crying. I boiled her an egg with some toast for lunch, but she usually left it beside the couch untouched.

She showed me her scar that extended most of the way across her swollen abdomen; it was red and ugly, latticed with stitch marks on either side.

"It all went down the sink in the operating room," she sobbed. "My body is dying, and it never lived."

I sat in the comfy chair and tried to finish *Gone with the Wind*. I longed to be Mammy in the story. She would know what to do. After several days of this, Blanche said, "Go home. If you stay here you will only learn to hate me."

"I will never hate you," I managed to blurt out in my anguished state.

"Go home," she repeated and turned her face to the wall. So I got on the streetcar and went home, devastated by my loss.

Blanche finally got better, but she seemed sad and uninterested in her home and the activities she had always enjoyed. This was not the same person I had skated with in Loring Park. She put on weight, although she did not seem to be eating, and she was usually tired.

When Christmas came, she managed to put up the tree, put out the manger scene, and cook the ham as usual. But there was not her former excitement in doing this. When we opened our gifts, Freddy had an unusual number of beautifully wrapped packages under the tree for her. He proudly said he had been keeping them in the trunk of the car so she wouldn't find them. She was still opening gifts after the rest of us were finished. There was perfume, bath salts, hand lotion, and scented soap. The largest package was a beautiful blue bathrobe. "I must have B.O.," she remarked sadly. Freddy's face fell. I could see how much he wanted to please her.

My life continued as usual in Mrs. H.'s home, except that I made a new friend, Paula, who lived in the neighborhood. Before long, we became best friends, and I spent many hours with her in her home. Her parents liked me and sometimes even invited me for dinner. They had a big house, and apparently were "the right kind of people," so Mother let me go.

Once, Paula's mother was away, and Paula's father took the two of us downtown to the Curtis Hotel for dinner. We were twelve years old, but he treated us like ladies, and we behaved elegantly.

Paula liked to ice-skate, and we would go together on the bus to the Minneapolis indoor skating arena. I loved to ice-skate and going skating with Paula was even better. I was surprised that Mother continued to go along with this, but I didn't ask questions and just enjoyed myself.

One Sunday, they invited me to go to church with them. I had not gone to church for a long time. I still missed going to that warm, nurturing Congregational church.

Any fears of the repetition of the Bible school experience evaporated as soon as I entered St. Mark's Episcopal Cathedral. The first thing I noticed was that there was no tank in the front. Instead, there was a beautiful altar, like the Congregational Church altar, except it was adorned with richly colored fabric. A gold cross, carefully centered on a white cloth, captured center stage on the altar. Richly colored stained glass windows surrounded the wall behind the altar. I had never seen stained glass, and I was awestruck by its beauty.

The organ was playing, and its majestic music filled my very being with reverence and longing. As we took our place in a pew, I was overpowered by the feeling I had come home.

There were small padded benches near the floor inviting those who wished to kneel and pray. I knelt and a prayer poured from my heart. The service began with a hymn and a procession. The minister (I soon learned he was called a priest) went to the altar, and he actually knelt as well. He read beautiful prayers, and we followed along from books in each pew. Sometimes everyone read aloud together. I thought that if Reverend Gregory knew about this, he would certainly do it this way, too. But what would Mother say about this? Were these our kind of people? I seriously doubted that they were.

I began going to church with Paula's family nearly every Sunday. They invited Mother to come along, but she was too busy. But she seemed happy that I was going. Strangely, she seemed to still think that these were our kind of people.

The terrible incidences with Mr. and Mrs. H. continued. Blanche's surgery threatened to drain my soul. Mother's abusive behaviors continued. I would have been ridiculed or put down if I shared any of my outward activities of growing up. She simply wasn't up to it. I had learned this in my struggles to make the apron. My life at school became a secret. My life at home became even more of a secret. Paula's parents made gentle inquiries but did not press me to confide in them. I spent as much time as I could with Paula in their home. And I now found that I could pray. The three things I could do in secret were read, write, and pray. This carried me through.

"The world may be coming to an end," exclaimed Freddy. It was a Sunday afternoon at their house, and we were sitting by the radio listening to the news of the detonation of the first atomic bomb. I felt my blood running cold through my body. "World without end," Blanche assured Freddy, quoting from the Apostle's Creed they said in church. I was comforted by Blanche's words as this news continued to unfold. World War II was soon over. With other children on our block, I took spoons and pans out in the street and beat them together as we all shouted loudly and joyfully.

"I wonder how long it will take them to build it all up again," I yearned in my naïve way, as I looked at the pictures of devastated towns and cities in the newspaper.

Soon after the war, I could see that Mother was under a strain at her work. There were new procedures and office equipment that she resisted. They asked her to take a correspondence course. She did her homework every week and mailed it in. It was fun for me to have Mother going to school. She got her papers back in the mail each week, and she nearly always got a perfect score. One time, she missed a question and was marked down a bit. This worried her. She dwelt on this, rather than on all the rest of the papers that were perfect. Things were changing at work. "Politics" was the way she described it.

Chapter 6

Mother sat down beside me one evening and popped the question as I was in my bed, reading. "How would you like to go to boarding school?"

"I'd like that," I replied with enthusiasm. I knew about boarding schools from the English novels I had been reading. Then Mother dropped the bomb.

"How would you like for me to go with you?"

"I wouldn't like that at all," I managed to reply. I thought perhaps she was joking, but that seemed an unlikely way for Mother to act.

"We're going," she said, closing the conversation. "I have already ordered your uniform." Mother had accepted a job as the school secretary at an Episcopal boarding school in Sioux Falls, South Dakota.

The good news was we were leaving the H.'s. The bad news was that I wasn't leaving Mother. The bad news was that we were leaving Blanche and Freddy. The bad news was that I was leaving Paula. The good news was that this had promise of being a change from the way we were living in Minneapolis. So off we went.

My first glimpse of what would be our home for the next five and a half years was from a cab sweeping us up a long graveled driveway. Before we had even turned into the driveway, a large rectangular sign commanded the view: All Saints School for Girls. We drove past a large expanse of snow-encrusted lawn, sloping down to the street.

Then I saw the school. My eyes widened, and my mouth dropped open. It looked like a huge country mansion in those English novels, but it was the largest mansion I could have imagined. The building was tall, yet sprawling and made of large rectangles of stone. I saw tall skinny chimneys, fat pointed towers, and even a round domed cupola on the roof. A steel fire escape zigzagged to the ground from a third-story window.

We entered into a long, wide hall with high ceilings. The hall ended in a rotunda at one end and opened to a beautiful chapel on the other. We stood by an imposing staircase leading I knew not where. Opposite this staircase was a hall leading to the largest classroom I had ever seen with row upon row of desks fastened to the floor. I was told that this was the study hall. A short, round lady who said she was the housemother had appeared.

"I'll show you your room; it's on the third floor," she cautioned. As eager as I was to see what was up that stairway, I walked slowly behind her as she was out of breath by the time we even reached the second floor. "The younger girl's rooms are up here," she managed to tell me as she puffed along.

We went down a narrow corridor, and then I saw my room. It was tiny and painted a bright pink that assaulted my eyes. A sink stood in the corner, and a miniature alcove covered by a curtain was the closet. A bed, dresser, and small desk and chair completed the room. And it was my own room—my very own room—and the first room I had ever had all to myself. Mother's room was way down on the second floor. The bathing ritual was over forever.

I was instantly immersed into the life of the school. It surprised me that it was so small. There were only twenty-seven girls in the high school and twelve in the junior high. The majority of the girls were boarders, but some were town girls who lived in Sioux Falls. There were grade-school girls as well, but they were town girls. We all wore uniforms with dark blue skirts, white cotton blouses, and red wool blazer jackets. Some of the girls resented the uniform. They longed for their own pretty outfits in their tiny closets, but these were strictly for after-school occasions. The most popular girls complained the most loudly. I liked the feeling of belonging the uniform gave me, even though the bright red was not becoming to my red hair and pale complexion. It was the most grown up outfit Mother had ever allowed me to wear.

I soon discovered the large dining room that occupied the entire basement space directly under the chapel. Bright flowered wallpaper made a welcoming contrast to the sea of white tablecloths, no-nonsense chairs, and big, round tables.

In addition to this spacious main building, there were two other buildings on the campus containing classrooms, a gymnasium, music and art rooms, and an auditorium. The buildings were connected by dimly lighted underground tunnels. We used these to walk between the buildings during the cold South Dakota winters.

Every morning, directly after breakfast, a teacher led us on a walk around the neighborhood. Since we didn't have to walk outside to go to school, the fresh air and exercise were preparation for the day. No one could leave the campus at any time without a teacher or a housemother.

After the walk, we had a morning prayer service in the chapel. The chapel was beautiful, with Tiffany stained glass windows giving a soft light to the semi-circular wall behind the altar. Brass candlesticks gleamed in the morning sun. Each pew had benches for kneeling and books for praying. It seemed to me an exquisite miniature of the Cathedral in Minneapolis.

I looked forward to chapel time secretly because it was not popular to admit that you liked chapel. Sometimes the bishop came and led the service. He had two daughters who were town girls at the school. He had a tendency to single me out, indicating to others how pious, well behaved, and studious he thought I was. This was disturbing. The very best way to be ridiculed by the other girls was to be "bishop's pet." But I found his attention attractive in a frightening sort of way. There were no other men anywhere in my life. There were lots of mother figures at the school but no father figures. My mother, with her will of steel, made sure she was the top mother figure for me.

Most of the teachers lived with us, occupying rooms along our various corridors. Besides teaching, they chaperoned our various outings off campus, ate three meals a day with us, took turns monitoring our nightly homework study hall, and spent time with us on weekends just socializing. The majority of them were just out of college, but they were, for the most part, excellent teachers.

I loved all the activity and the constant company of other girls. At night, after lights out, the girls on my corridor sat on the floor in our doorways talking way into the night. If we heard a teacher's step on the stairs, there was plenty of time to scurry back to our beds.

After school, we skied and sledded on the sloping lawn leading down to the street. An area was flooded for ice-skating, and I quickly and joyfully found my skates. In spring and fall, we played tennis, badminton, archery, and croquet, or we just enjoyed being outside. Inside, someone was always pounding on the piano in the girls' lounge, and we practiced crazy dances and imagined we were flirting with boys.

Each girl was required to go to the school doctor for a physical examination, so I was soon taken downtown to see the doctor. All seemed to be well with me, but he stuck a patch inside my lower arm to screen for TB. He told me not to take the patch off until the next day and watch the spot for a few days to make sure no redness or swelling appeared. Within two days, the area was red, swollen, and inflamed. I was terrified. I just knew I was very sick and would have to go away to a sanitarium.

My terror increased by the hour. I told Mother, but she acted unconcerned. When it came to any physical discomfort, she often said I exaggerated its importance. I couldn't sleep and lay awake desperately crying, muffling sobs into my pillow so no one would hear.

The following day, after another night of secret weeping, I was taken back to the doctor for a chest X-ray. It showed that I didn't have TB. When the doctor told me, I began to tremble all over and my legs gave way. The nurse quickly brought me a chair. The doctor gently explained that I had antibodies in my body against TB. That was the reason for the skin reaction. The antibodies were good and could help prevent the disease. He said my X-rays showed small, healed scars on my lungs. Those antibodies had been successful in arresting the disease.

Relief and gratitude flooded through my body. It was like a magic wand had been waved over it. My legs felt strong, and I stood up, inwardly embracing my precious healthy self. My future beckoned me once more.

When I got back to school, Mother came to my room. "Your father died of TB." She stood close to the door as she blurted out this revelation. "You were first tested when you were three. You had the scars then."

My legs got that weak feeling again, and I sat down on the bed, hoping I wouldn't start shaking. Until then, I had not known how you died. Mother continued standing close to the door.

"I have healed scars in my lungs too." She looked confused as if she were trying to put together a puzzle and couldn't find all the pieces. "I found out when you were three as well."

I looked at her face for as long as I dared. Why was she confused? What were those missing puzzle pieces? Were they the ways she didn't know how to look at me and talk to me about this terrible time that shaped our lives? I longed to be able to find the pieces for her—and for me as well.

After Mother left, I sat for a long time feeling how you had died, sealed away from everyone you loved and everyone who loved you. Sealed away from your home, work, wife, and baby. When I grew up, I would need to unearth my buried anger at you for dying and leaving me with Mother. But at that moment, I felt angry at the TB and felt an overwhelming anguish for your suffering, for what happened to you— the anguish of your aborted life.

What would have happened if our TB had not been arrested? If I had died, would Mother's life been better, more salvageable in her way of thinking? What would have happened to me if she had gotten the disease and been shut away? Who would have cared for me? Aunt Lida, Faye, and Arlene, I am certain. What would have happened if Mother had died? I would have been adopted by Uncle Raymond and Aunt Gertrude and would have grown up in a home, immersed in the extended Elliott family. But then I would not have known Blanche and Freddy, or Mother, for that matter. What would have happened if both Mother and I had died? Our small branch of the family tree would be gone forever. There are so many interesting "ifs."

All too soon, my seventh grade year ended. I was thriving on the energy and atmosphere of the school. Perhaps I was also affected by my heightened awareness of sickness and death and the precious nature of life. In any case, I was doing well. I had become used to the bright pink walls, and my own room had become my little home. I was making friends, I liked all my teachers, and my report card was excellent. Everyone praised Mother for having such a lovely daughter, and when Mother was happy, I was happy.

The school year ended with graduation exercises for the five seniors followed by a festive lunch for everyone. After tearful good-byes, girls were shuttled off to the airport, train station, or bus depot. Some parents picked up their daughters. They were driven off, waving from open car windows, already having entered that other world, the world of home and family.

Suddenly the moment came when I had said the last good-bye. I walked alone along the empty corridors, feeling like I was stranded alone on a planet. I was the only one with no place to go. I was isolated and unconnected with anyone. I feared I was going insane. I ran to Mother's office, desperately needing to make contact with her. She was bent over her typewriter.

"Janet, I'm very busy," she chided me. "It's good that the girls are finally gone. I can have some peace and quiet to do my work."

Although it was only early afternoon, I filled a bathtub with hot water, took off my clothes, and slid down in the tub until the water covered my whole body way up to my neck. I stayed there the rest of the afternoon. As the water cooled, I replenished it with more hot water.

The next day, Mother and I began living a summer life, which would be our routine for five summers. I moved down to the second floor near Mother's room. Sometimes a housemother or the headmistress lived in other parts of the building. A janitor lived in a basement apartment. He had epileptic seizures and went off his medicine in the summer. I would enter a room unexpectedly and find him in the midst of a grand mal seizure. I was helpless and afraid. I always felt uneasy in the emptiness of the school. The huge building would creak in mysterious ways. There was a rumor among the girls that Bishop Hare's ghost walked the halls in the night. Bishop Hare was the first bishop of South Dakota, and he had founded the school in 1885.

During the summer, I was free to go off campus. I made friends with several other town girls, and we rode our bicycles, went swimming in the local pool, went to the movies on Saturday afternoon, and just spent time hanging out, talking at their houses or at what I came to think of in the summer as my school. They liked to come there on hot days because the stone building was always cool.

I discovered the public library and checked out armloads of books—as many as my bicycle basket would hold. I also spent hot afternoons reading in the school library. It was a large, inviting room in the main building, and I had all the books to myself. The solitude and quiet seemed more inviting there, not lonely or fearful.

I discovered a sex education book down on a low shelf in a corner. I knew where babies grew, and I knew they came out down below someplace in a very painful way. (Mother had impressed this on me many times.) From the stirrings in my own body, confirmed by talks with girl friends, my sense was that sex and marriage were very pleasurable. But the book supplied a missing link in my knowledge when it described sexual intercourse. I could not imagine anyone ever doing that.

When I was six, a teenaged boy had lifted me down into a large window well. He sat on the ground, unzipped his pants, and asked me to watch him as he squeezed and rubbed this mysterious appendage until something squirted out the end. Then he zipped it back up and lifted me out of the well, and I quickly ran home.

My thirteen-year-old mind simply could not get itself around the facts confronting me in the book.

Chapter 7

"That child needs a bra."

We had just arrived in Buffalo, New York, to visit Aunt Rene and Uncle Mac. Aunt Rene was Mother's other sister. She had been watching us as we walked up the platform from the train. These were her first words of greeting. I instantly had Aunt Rene on my side. Very soon, we all went shopping.

Mother bought me the bra, and Aunt Rene bought me two very nice dresses. I enlisted Aunt Rene's help in getting a new bathing suit. The one Mother insisted I could still wear was made for a child, and my grown-up places had a habit of escaping in embarrassing ways. My new bathing suit was one piece, lovely and curvaceous in a soft peach color that I thought was perfect. Aunt Rene also let me wear her fancy nightgown. I would parade around the house in it until Uncle Mac protested to Aunt Rene, and she told me to put on a robe. I put on her robe, which was just as fancy as her nightgown and smelled of perfume, but apparently, my curves were sufficiently veiled.

For this two-week visit, Aunt Rene had the upper hand. I was exhilarated. There was a near meltdown when Mother didn't want me to wear one of my new dresses to Niagara Falls. For my thirteenth birthday, I wanted to celebrate becoming a teenager by looking really festive, and Uncle Mac was taking us to a restaurant for dinner. Mother insisted the spray from the falls might get my dress wet. I began to cry. Again, Aunt Rene came to the rescue.

"Oh, look who's crying on her special birthday." She put an arm around me, and I cried harder. "I have never seen the falls get anyone wet." She insisted with the authority of a local native. "You must wear your pretty dress on your birthday." There wasn't another word out of Mother.

Shoes designed to look like ballet slippers were the fashion among teen-aged girls. Of course, I wanted a pair. Naturally, Mother said no, stating that they were a waste of money and bad for my feet. After the bra, the dresses, and the bathing suit, I was content not to push the ballet slipper issue.

One day, toward the end of our visit, out of nowhere, Mother looked up from the magazine she was pretending to read and made a formal announcement.

"You may have the ballet slippers."

"Why?" I rejoiced in amazement.

"Because I know how much I would have liked to have had ballet slippers when I was thirteen."

"Oh, thank you, thank you, thank you."

My voice rose in a canticle of thanksgiving. Thanksgiving for the astonishing gift of the ballet slippers to be sure, but more importantly, thanksgiving for her momentary connection with my newly minted, fragile, teenaged self. I wish with all my heart that you had been there.

In September, the girls poured back into the school, and I felt assured that this migration would occur every year. I moved back to the third floor, this time to a room painted a pleasing pale yellow. It had a view of the play field, which in winter was the skating rink.

I was thirteen, an eighth-grader now, and the older, wild girls made overtures to include me in their group. These girls talked of summer romances that included beer, cars, and heavy necking. They defied school rules, sneaking off to smoke in a corner of campus referred to as Happy Hollow. At night, boys from town drove by the school, calling their names, and they would sneak down the fire escape to meet them. The headmistress, who only lasted that one year, called a special assembly and announced to the entire school that she was in charge, and everyone would learn this if she had to break every bone in our bodies.

I was exhilarated by the danger of being with these girls, relishing their secrets as we piled on a bed, talking, basking in the promise of being free, belligerent, and wild. But it frightened me. As much as I craved this inclusion, deep down, this wasn't who I was. It could take over and smother me. The trouble was that I didn't know who I was. Was there a middle ground between "bishop's pet" and belligerent and wild?

Mother was fueled by the headmistress's threatened massacre. She had quickly sniffed out my potential connections to the wild and belligerent and told me if I didn't shape up, she would break every bone in my body personally. I knew if she accidentally missed one, she would turn me over to the headmistress to finish the job.

In the spring, I was confirmed with three other girls in the school chapel. In the Episcopal Church, the bishop does the confirmation service. I was relieved to learn that it wouldn't be the "bishop's pet" bishop, but another retired bishop who didn't know very many of us.

It was a cold, windy March day. The chapel was drafty. Bereft of my wool blazer jacket, I shivered in my white cotton dress uniform, which was our special garb for important chapel occasions. Those being confirmed wore white veils, giving the occasion the importance of a wedding. The organ played and everyone sang "Breathe on Me Breath of God." The bishop laid his hands on my head and prayed the words:

> *Defend, Oh Lord, this thy child with thy heavenly grace,*
> *That she may continue thine forever*
> *And daily increase in thy Holy Spirit more and more*
> *Until she comes unto thy everlasting kingdom. Amen.*

I fell in love with God. This love affair had to be very secret. It could not be shared with any school friend. I would be rejected as pious and prudish, and any hope of finding my own voice in this milieu of cliques and groups would be cruelly dashed.

There was another reason for secrecy. Mother saw something new in me that she couldn't find a way to get a hold of. She couldn't mold it to her liking. She had access to every part of me she wanted, but she couldn't get to this. For the rest of her life, it would drive her into a frenzy.

She took me to Sunday school to learn to be good, obedient, and polite; mind my mother; and meet the right people. She did this job well. She brought me to this Episcopal school to keep me very close to her and because, in her mind, Episcopalians were the upper class, those right people, successful owners and managers of the power and wealth of the country. Episcopalians had beautiful homes with maids to do the housework. Her expectation of my confirmation was that it would seal our membership in the company of the right people. Can you understand this?

Many years later, on a visit to Portland, I stood high on a hill outside Trinity Episcopal Cathedral. In the late nineteenth century, lumber barons, early wealthy Episcopal settlers from the East Coast, built this church. The Multnomah Golf and Country Club occupied an equally beautiful site next door. Although this is now a diverse and worship-centered congregation, I was told that, in these early days, one belonged to Trinity Episcopal Church and the Multnomah Golf Club to ensure acceptance into the city's socially elite.

I looked out on the city that stretched across the river to the place where your first home had been. I could imagine Mother there looking up to the top of this hill and craving what she imagined she saw there. She was on a mission.

The summer after eighth grade, I visited Blanche and Freddy in Minneapolis for three wonderful weeks. To my delight, I also visited Paula, and we spent the day in serious girl talk, catching up on each other's happenings. It had been a year and a half since we had been together. Paula seemed so grown up and free. Paula and her family wanted me to stay an extra week in Minneapolis and spend it at their house, but Mother did not go along with this plan.

Blanche had joined a Book of the Month Club and was eager for me to read her new books. I read way into the night in their big guestroom bed, enjoying *The Shoes of the Fisherman*, *The Grapes of Wrath*, and *The Good Earth*. In the morning, I slept as late as I wanted. Blanche always made bacon and eggs for my breakfast, no matter how late I got up. Dinner usually included green beans and corn on the cob. Each evening, at 10:00, there was Cedric Adams and cheese, pretzels, and Pepsi-Cola in the kitchen with Freddy.

Blanche and I washed our hair each Saturday, and I curled her hair after I curled mine. This involved coiling each small strand of hair around my finger and pinning it close to the scalp with bobby pins. We wrapped our heads in scarves all day as our hair dried. Then we combed it out. At dinner, Freddy admired our beautiful curls. Blanche let me wear lipstick the whole time I was there.

On Sunday, we went to the Lutheran Church where Freddy had been confirmed when he was a boy. Later, in our talks, Blanche told me how much going to church meant to her. She said God was there, and it was a place where she felt that she really belonged.

Something was happening under the surface of our lives in a gradual, subtle way. Mother was snubbing Blanche. Blanche and Freddy's ordinary way of life was beneath what she imagined for me. During our infrequent visits, Mother talked about all the rich and Eastern college-educated people who made up our life in Sioux Falls, the large homes she had infrequently visited, and the important businessmen who were on the board of the school.

During our boarding school years, we always went to Minneapolis for Christmas, but Mother could only stay a few days, making the excuse that she had to get back to work. During the visits, she seemed bored. The excitement of learning about social happenings and news of important people whose lives she observed from the outside were most important to her. We no longer spent Thanksgiving or Easter in Minneapolis, and of course, Sunday dinners were over 200 miles away. Sometimes I stayed longer at Christmastime after

Mother went back, but she always seemed uneasy until I was back in school, totally under her strong wing.

Chapter 8

The September migration of girls back into the empty corridors reassured me that good things were about to happen. I was a freshman in high school, with a room on the second floor.

School discipline problems had smoothed out. The most wild and belligerent girls had either managed to graduate or had not come back. Miss Dorland, the new headmistress, genuinely liked each and every girl. She instilled in us a joy in living and an appreciation of learning that I carry with me today. She also taught Latin and French classes. She took over chaperoning the morning walk, a job all the teachers hated, and as a result, developed a consistent rapport with us as we walked. This was characteristic of the way she ran the school. She often stayed at the school during the summer, so she and I became especially good friends.

We changed classes and had a different teacher for each subject now. I continued to do very well in most of my classes all through high school. You would have been proud of me, Dad. (Now I know what feels right to call you. I'll call you Dad. I am imagining giving you a big hug as I say your special name.)

I even liked algebra, and later geometry, even though math had been far from my favorite subject. I decided in grade school that it was boring and turned off my brain whenever I encountered it. I also struggled with math because I changed schools so often in grade school. I missed some basics along the way. I still count on my fingers and make mistakes with the multiplication tables. But this was a different way of thinking and reasoning than I had experienced earlier, and here I was getting A's in math. I was so proud of myself.

Learning Latin and French were great adventures, I am sure in part because of Miss Dorland's wonderful teaching methods.

My English class was even better. Miss Dick, my teacher for all four years of high school, introduced me to the world of American and English classical literature. She took us to see Shakespearian plays at the local college and more contemporary plays at the Sioux Falls community theater. She also taught us to write. In her classes, we diagrammed sentences, improved our vocabularies, and corrected our spelling errors. Most importantly, she gave me a beginning appreciation and confidence in putting my thoughts and feelings on paper that has lasted all my life.

Miss Dick was just out of college and like a big sister to us. She had a serious boyfriend, and she told us so much about her life. She had grown up in North Dakota and, for some reason, was brought up by her grandmother. Her boyfriend broke up with her, and he broke our hearts as well as hers. One summer she went to England, and later she told us in class all about what she had seen and done. I longed to go there. She brought us gifts. Mine was a little statue of Dickens' Mr. Pickwick that still sits on my bookcase.

All through high school—and college, too, for that matter—I disliked history classes. This is the only place I never did well. In retrospect, I wonder if it was because my own sense of time and place in the world were not firmly established. Was I simply not ready to learn about other places, times, and events? The history teacher reported that I was a daydreamer and had a bad attitude toward my work. This was true.

In science class, I liked biology, even dissecting earthworms. Then our teacher got a dead cat preserved in formaldehyde for us to dissect. That was fascinating, although it did take some getting used to. I liked seeing all the inside parts of a body. I thought it best not to tell Mother about the cat or earthworms. Later, by contrast, I found chemistry disappointing and boring—just tables of facts to learn and stuff in test tubes.

Everyone had a religion class once a week. Remember that I secretly loved chapel? Well, religion was very boring. The good thing was that it had no tests or homework.

P.E. was not usually my favorite subject. We always did calisthenics that only made me sweat. I was stiff and not as limber as many of the other girls who moved and bent with such grace.

But I excelled in girl's basketball. I could run, dribble the ball, dodge, and throw those baskets with remarkable skill and grace. I was tall, which helped with throwing baskets, but it still surprised me how much I enjoyed the game and how well I did. In P.E. class, we had two teams, the purples and the golds, which were our school colors. Often I was captain of the golds.

You would not be proud of me, Dad; I was terrible at softball. I know you loved ball games. I couldn't get the timing to bat the ball, either left- or right-handed, no matter how hard the teacher tried to help me. And I was afraid to catch the ball because I didn't want to hurt my hand. Pretty bad, huh?

Every girl in high school was required to be in the choir. We sang for special services in the chapel, where the Sioux Falls community was invited on All Saints' Day, Easter, and during the Christmas season. Mother said I took after you because, she explained, you couldn't sing. I don't know if that is true or not, but I was always tense in choir.

I was a second soprano, which meant carrying a part in the middle between the sopranos and altos. I was never sure of myself. I wanted to sing soprano because I could sing the melody, but that was not going to happen. I wonder if you really couldn't sing.

Another teacher, Mrs. Close, was a quiet mentor for me in these high school years. First and foremost, she taught algebra and geometry, but then she succeeded in expanding the curriculum in an important way.

"Aren't these girls going to get married and keep house someday?" she repeatedly asked Miss Dorland. Miss Dorland, being single—an "old maid" as we called it then—had never thought of this as an education concern. But Mrs. Close was a mother and homemaker and had majored in home economics in college. She lived in town; her husband was also a teacher but at the public high school. She had two teenaged children who went to public high school. They went to the Congregational Church. Mrs. Close was a maverick in our school environment.

She got permission to offer a class called Home Management. It was made clear that this class was strictly an elective because this school was for the purpose of college preparation. We still had to take our full allotment of credit classes at the same time.

There was not space or equipment to offer a true home economics class, but Mrs. Close did the best she could. She brought in two portable sewing machines during the time we had a sewing project. She arranged for us to use the school kitchen for the times we cooked. We had a textbook entitled *Your Home and You*. I still have it on my shelf. For me, it was the blueprint for the first day of creation. We learned about meal planning, shopping, budgeting, and housecleaning to be sure. We all got recipe boxes and began a file of recipes. Each of us sewed a garment. I made a pair of cotton pajamas that made me so proud. We learned to knit and could knit during class discussions. I made a pair of argyle socks, following the pattern that required successfully keeping track of multiple skeins of yarn.

But Mrs. Close taught us so much more. She taught us simply by her presence. She told us about her own family; what they did at home, school, and church and in the community; and the ways she cared for them. This gave me an idea of a real home and its future possibilities for me. We learned the special ways that each of us was attractive, and we talked about the colors we should wear to bring out our natural beauty. We could imagine a world beyond the world of the school uniform.

I was the tallest girl in the school; I was five feet eight inches by the time I was in eighth grade. This fact, along with my red hair, that I had yet to appreciate, made me feel awkward and different. And I was the only girl who had no other home and had her mother at school. This made me feel even more different. Mrs. Close cut through all of this. She also had red hair and was attractive. She told me her daughter had red hair, and she was the prom queen at her high school. She told me that I was smart, beautiful, and very capable and to look forward to college because then many people would be as tall as I was. My life would expand in wonderful ways. Mrs. Close encouraged my own vision and helped me prepare for my own future. She was pivotal in my life, a vessel of hope and encouragement.

Just as I think of Blanche when I reflect on my childhood, I think of Miss Dorland, Miss Dick, and Mrs. Close when I think of my adolescence. These women formed and grounded me and filled me with all that I took with me as I grew up.

You, the soldier

You when you met mother

Mother when she met you

Courting days

Safe in your arms, let's go for a ride.

Mother with her baby; happy at last

Mary Marie and I with
Freddie and Blanche

Congregational Church Children's
Choir. I am the last girl on the right.

Girl Scout troup in Minneapolis; I'm in the middle.

All Saints School in Sioux Falls, South Dakota

I am reflecting on everything.

My confirmation

My wonderful teacher, Mrs. Close and some of her girls.
I am next to her on the left.

With Mother on my high
school Graduation Day.

Canterbury Club: Bill is fourth from left;
I am the readhead in the front row.

With Uncle Raymond on my wedding day.

Bill and i begin our new life together.

Outside our Puyallup apartment a week before Mark's birth

Phil, Andy and Mark with Grandma Cele, summer 1966.
In central Oregon for Aunt Mae's and Uncle Bill's 50th wedding celebration.

John and Uncle Raymond throwing rocks in the Umatilla River, 1968.

The Family 1970, back row: Mark, Phil
Front row: John, Janet, Andy and Bill

1979, nearly all grown up. Back row: John, Andy, Bill
Front row: Mark, Janet, and Phil. (and Sam, for 16 years our beloved pet)

Chapter 9

The summer I turned fifteen, Mother and I went on that familiar train ride back to Portland for a visit. Aunt Lida and Uncle Earl met us at the train and were startled to see the tall slender teenager that I had become. They had been stuck in the images they carried of me when I was small. Now my bra was like a familiar second skin on my shapely body. I wore a peasant blouse with a fashionable dirndl skirt, and guess what else? My now well-worn ballet slippers. They rejoiced that I still had my red hair, so reminiscent of your mother.

"She looks like the Potter side of the Elliott family!" they exclaimed. I learned your mother's maiden name was Potter.

Cousins, now grown up and married with children, came from all over town to see us. There was a large family picnic at Dodge Park that included a cousin's softball game, and this was apparently a tradition at family picnics. I volunteered to play fielder. It was usually a safe position in gym class at school because hardly anyone hit a ball that far. But Aunt Lida's son Bill Ralston slugged a bullet of a ball right toward me. I was determined to catch it. It managed to hit one of my hands and sprained my thumb.

So there I sat for the rest of the afternoon, the center of attention with my thumb packed in ice. Would you believe that Bill actually blamed himself for hitting the ball so hard, and Uncle George's daughter, Maxine, the other fielder, blamed herself for letting me run for the ball? I know you were so good in these family softball games. You would have been ashamed of me.

During this visit, I grew up fast, in Aunt Lida's estimation. One afternoon, she and I were home alone. She wept as she told me about the time we lived in Portland, recalling your delight in contrast to Mother's outrage at my birth. She told of the time we lived with her, your struggle to get well, and your death. She told me our tragic story. She lived it as your sister, but she lived it with you, Mother, and me as well. The pieces of this story came together for me then.

Aunt Lida and Uncle Earl drove us to central Oregon. As we went along the Mt. Hood highway, Aunt Lida reminisced about taking me there the Christmas you were in the hospital, and she recalled how I threw up all along the way.

The central Oregon relatives, your sisters and brothers, were overjoyed to see us. We stayed with Aunt Mae in the home where you lived as a boy. That was when Aunt Mae gave me the box with all the letters you wrote to her and your mother when you were in the army. I rode a horse on Uncle George's farm, where you rode horses as a boy.

Then we drove to Pendleton to see Uncle Raymond and Aunt Gertrude and their two children, who were now teenagers as well. Uncle Raymond was a manager in one of the local banks and Aunt Gertrude was a stay-at-home housewife and mother. It was a small town, and they seemed to know many people. The children went to public high school with dances, bands, and football games. On Friday evening, they gathered with friends at a teen hangout in town. It seemed like such a complete, ordinary life. It was like what I read about in books and saw in the movies—so unlike the unusual existence I had with Mother. I wanted to live like that.

Uncle Raymond gave me an especially long hug as we got in the car for Uncle Earl to drive us back to Portland. Was that hug from you? I think maybe it was.

Back in Portland, we said good-bye to all of those relatives and took the train to Seattle. There we visited Florence and Ed McKnight, who were close friends from your business years in Seattle and Portland. From as long as I could remember, I had referred to them as Uncle Ed and Auntie Florence. I thought of them as part of that distant family connection. They had a lovely home near the University of Washington and had friends over for dinner that Mother knew and enjoyed.

Larry McKnight, their son who went to college, took me to the movies. I felt very grown up. They drove us to Olympia to visit some people named Allison. They remembered you well and told me how wonderful you were. They must have been business friends, but by then they owned a well-known oyster restaurant in the town, and we had dinner there. I was treated as a grown up, lovely young lady this whole visit. I put on lipstick every day, and Mother couldn't find a graceful way to protest.

Amongst cousins, family, and family friends, I discovered boys that summer. I wondered how this new awareness would fit in with my life with Mother and school. We had few opportunities to be with boys at school.

Sometimes we had school dances, which were formal affairs. Boys from an approved list were invited to be our dates. Some of the boys really liked to come and were seriously dating girls at the school. One of my dates put his arm around me and kissed me on the cheek. Boys came up at other times to visit, and when we all went to church on Sunday, certain boys and girls would make a beeline for each other. There were still the boys who drove by the fire escape at night calling out vulgar names, but these were becoming fewer in number since Miss Dorland came. Aside from the kiss on the cheek, my connection with boys was distant, at best.

I also discovered men that summer—uncles, cousins, your business friends—all of whom adored me. And then there was Larry McKnight, who was twenty-one years old and took me to a movie in his car. There were no men at the school except for the janitor, the bishop, and a priest who taught the religion class. Uncle Freddy had been the only man in my life until that summer, and he too was a long way away.

But I came back from the trip connected with your family and friends in a new way. These were real people who knew me and saw me as a real person too.

The pictures and stories and letters had come to life.

My sophomore year began with the familiar return of everyone to the school. My two best friends were back, and since I didn't have to take history that year, my classes were going well.

But one morning, in early November, I was standing in the dining room after breakfast when everything began to look unreal. My eyes and my brain seemed disconnected. I told the housemother. Among her jobs was evaluating and treating complaints of sickness. She said I probably had the flu and to stay in bed for the day. I stayed in bed for several days, and this feeling did not go away. I got up and tried to go to class, but the feeling got even worse. In chapel, I was afraid I would lose my mind during the service, and I would disturb those around me as I left in a panic.

Finally, Mother took me to the doctor—the same doctor who had seen me through the TB scare. After careful examination, he told me there was nothing wrong with me. He went on to say that he had sometimes felt this way as a teenager, and it went away as he got older. It would go away for me as well. He prescribed a mysterious bottle of medicine for me to take for a week, explaining to Mother that this might help me.

As we walked home from the doctor, up the hill to the school, I wanted to cling to Mother, but I knew she wouldn't let me do that.

"What is that medicine?" I asked.

"It's something I took a long time ago." She had that look on her face again, like she couldn't put puzzle pieces together.

"Why did you take it?" I persisted.

"I don't want to talk about it," she replied.

Whatever the medicine was, it gave me permission to be sick.

The housemother checked my temperature every day. She brought my meals to my room. My teachers excused me from class, saying I could make up my work when I felt better. For a week, I didn't even read. Mostly, I just slept.

At last, I got up and tried to rejoin the world. But I didn't feel better. These feelings of everything seeming unreal continued to occur. They would come over me without warning—in the dining room, in chapel, in my classes. I would have to leave in the middle of breakfast, chapel, or schoolwork, causing an embarrassing and unacceptable disruption.

Everyone around me was beginning to feel puzzled and helpless. Could it be that I was faking or exaggerating these symptoms? I felt like I was shut up in a terrifying world of my own. No one could understand or reach me or make me well. Was I going insane? Would I be locked up forever?

One evening I went to Mother's room. I was desperate to tell her that I wasn't getting better. She met me at the door.

"Mother, I'm not better." I began to cry.

"Janet, I'm tired of this." I remember that she wore a frayed flannel nightgown with a tear in one sleeve.

"But, Mother…" I sobbed. I was desperate to convince her.

"I'm an old lady—you think of me for a change. You need to stop this, and you need to stop crying. You need to snap out of this, and snap out of it right now." She closed the door.

I stood alone in the hall outside her closed door. The walls seemed to be closing in on me on both sides, constricting me. I walked along these halls to my room and went to bed. It would be twenty years before I cried again.

From that time on, I moved in terror through my days, going through the motions, hiding the disconnection between my eyes and my brain, hiding my fear that I was going insane. When my terror compelled me to leave a room, I stayed there anyway, stiffening my body to keep myself in place. After a while, I got used to it and found I could bear it. It was a new way of being normal for me. I began to read and study again and got all A's on my report card that semester.

Every December, before the girls scattered for Christmas vacation, there was a traditional evening candlelight service. The chapel, fragrant with freshly cut greens and lighted only by candles, was packed with visitors. Folding chairs were set up along both sides of the large entrance hall, extending way back to the formal staircase. As the organ resounded its accompaniment, all the girls from first grade through high school processed into the chapel, carrying lighted candles and singing "O Come All Ye Faithful." We assembled at the front of the chapel and sang Christmas anthems and carols, woven in with the reading of the Christmas story from the Gospel of Luke.

Every year, the teachers selected a sophomore girl to do the reading of this scripture. That year, there were four of us in the class, and I was selected. There was no way I could get out of it. If, in even the slightest way, I revealed any of my sensations or fears, the school seemed into be a conspiracy. Everyone indicated to me that one simply closed ranks and forged on.

There was one bright spot. This meant that I didn't have to sing in the choir. I was fearful of being confined in a place in a performance, where, with all my tension, I could even more easily sing off-key.

We rehearsed over and over again. The choir was hounded into perfection. I was a good reader and had a strong voice. All I had to do was to get up and read the part of the scripture that was to come after each group of songs. Somehow, with all the focus on this upcoming event, my panic subsided some.

When the big evening arrived, my body was stiff and my hands were cold, but I felt strangely calm. As I read, the words began to have meaning for me. I remembered the manger scene in Blanche's home in Minneapolis. I remembered Mary Marie under the Christmas tree when I was four. I knew about miracles; I knew the story I was reading.

Afterward, so many people told me how well I had read. And remember that boy who kissed me on the cheek at the dance? Well, he came up to me. "That was a great job of reading," he managed to blurt out before he disappeared again into the crowd.

We went to Minneapolis for Christmas, and Blanche's familiar rituals had a calming effect on me. I felt better, and when we returned was eager to resume the familiar routine of school. When I got that disconnected feeling, I would wait it out in secret. Everyone around me seemed to think I was just fine. I wanted to keep it that way.

When summer came along with the familiar emptying of the school, I was frightened. Although I could go off campus now, and there were friends in town who were eager to do things with me, I panicked when I left the school. This happened even walking to the drug store to buy shampoo or *Seventeen* magazine. My heart raced with terror, my body stiffened, and I was sure I was going to fall over, go insane, and be locked away. I only felt comfort when I was inside the school, either in my room or curled up in a chair in the library reading a book. My friends called or came over, but I made excuses to stay by myself.

I was asked to take a regular babysitting job several blocks from the school, to sit with the baby two afternoons a week while the mother went out. This mother was an alumna of the school, a lovely lady who was one of Mother's "right people." By this time, Mother had had enough of what she described as my moping around and insisted that I take the job. It was all I could do to walk over to the house; such was my panic along the way. When I was left alone with the baby, I feared I would go insane and kill her. I sat outside in the backyard with her all afternoon because I felt it was safer there. No one knew how I was feeling, and it didn't seem to show. This mother thought I was doing a great job with the baby. Miss Dorland thought I was going through a teenage stage. I didn't know what Mother really thought, even though she passed it off as just moping.

What was causing my terrifying feelings and symptoms? It would be twenty years before I understood and was free at last to cry. A truth churned under the surface of our lives that escalated to a collision course as I emerged into a beautiful, independent teenaged girl. Mother and I hated each other. She hated me for being born. I hated her for the assaults on my helpless body, mind, and spirit that threatened to abort their very development. I was responding to the urgings of my growing self, which were cheering me on toward the woman I was to become. I was in competition with Mother and was terrified that I would lose.

There was something else—our grief. During the summer trip to Portland, I was old enough to feel my grief at what I lost when you died, the grief of our never knowing each other, the grief of all we both missed and would always miss for the rest of my life. I came back from Portland knowing my grief. Although I tried to hide it, Mother sensed it, and it threatened her. She only felt safe keeping the grief to herself, explaining it her way, managing it in the way she wanted it to be managed. I was intruding into an area where she was unprepared.

Partnered with our grief was this hate. Mother hated me, but she also hated you because of my birth and because you died. And I also hated you for dying; I didn't realize this for many years.

Something else I didn't realize for many years is that hate is the other side of love. The greater our love, the greater is our capacity to hate; they are two sides of the same coin. We both loved you wildly, and we both loved each other, but each day, we caused each other grief We both hated, we both grieved, and yes, we both loved, but in very separate ways we couldn't allow ourselves to understand.

Chapter 10

The following summer, I spent four weeks on a cattle ranch in Gettysburg, South Dakota. You must be asking, "How in the world did a daughter of your mother go to a cattle ranch?" It was home to Barbara, one of my school friends. She and her parents invited me for a visit. I didn't think Mother would let me go because she felt she couldn't stay at the school by herself, but these were those "right kind" of people she talked about. Barbara's father was a member of the South Dakota House of Representatives.

Barbara and her mother picked me up when they came to Sioux Falls for Barbara's orthodontist appointment. The plan was for me to stay for only a week. But something wonderful happened, and I stayed for a month. Once I got there, Barbara's mother said she couldn't bring me back until they came for Barbara's next orthodontist appointment and that was in four weeks. Mother could do nothing about it.

This sprawling ranch sat in the wilderness of the South Dakota prairie. When I stood on the back porch of the large white house looking out across the terrain, the property lines were too far in the distance to see. Grazing land for cattle and wheat fields spread across miles, where winter food for the cattle was grown and harvested, something that was essential for the long South Dakota winters. Nearer the house, barns sheltered the cattle and sheds stored tractors, trucks, and all the mysterious tools and equipment necessary to a ranch. Dusty roads lead everywhere, and no grass covered the ground anywhere. For me, this was an exciting new world to explore.

The large, modern house was well insulated from the dust in the summer and the snow and cold in the winter. The spacious kitchen had an extra large stove and ovens and a huge refrigerator. A large stairway led up to the bedrooms. I shared Barbara's room, sleeping with her in her double bed. We could talk well into the night.

I was in teenage heaven. Barbara had two teenaged brothers, and more teenaged boys came every day to work on the ranch. They were harvesting wheat, and everyone came in from the field for a big dinner at noon. I helped with food preparation, setting the table, and even dishwashing. I enjoyed every minute, and Barbara's mother said I was a fast learner. Her parents liked having me there because Barbara's attitude about all this work improved some when seen through my eyes. For Barbara, these had been just routine chores that became harder during harvest times. She appreciated my company.

As we worked, Barbara's mother told me stories about their earlier lives on the ranch. She told about the dust bowl in the early 1930s when strong winds blew the topsoil across miles and miles of Midwestern farmland, leaving crops destroyed and animals starving. This was in the early days of their marriage, and she remembered looking out her kitchen window and not being able to see the barn because of the thick dust blowing across their prairie. The dust crept in through cracks in the house, and she put wet clothes over her baby's nose to keep it from filling up with the dust. For me, this was *Little House on the Prairie* brought to life.

I learned to milk a cow. I couldn't fill my pail as fast as the others, but I was good enough that I helped with the milking every evening. The pails of milk were brought into the kitchen, and this fresh milk was poured through a device called a separator that divided the milk from the cream.

Afterward, the separator had to be washed and thoroughly sterilized to be ready for the next evening's milking. Washing the separator was a job no one liked, especially because it came at the end of a long day of work. I became adept at washing the separator, and Barbara's mother entrusted me with this job nearly every evening.

First, I disassembled all the pieces and scrubbed each piece thoroughly with a small brush dipped in hot soapy water. Then water was repeatedly poured over these pieces until they were thoroughly rinsed. The last step was sterilizing it by pouring boiling water over each part. After they were air-dried, the device had to be reassembled, ready for the next milking. The milk was sold to a local dairy that carefully checked for contaminants. If the milk didn't pass inspection, it would no longer be bought from this farm. Washing the separator perfectly was an important job. I took it on with pride.

Of course, much of this work energy came from being around all the boys. It came from a fascination with Barbara's father too. In the early morning, he called all of our names from the bottom of the stairs, followed with the shout, "Hit the deck." His presence was everywhere. He managed the farm and the family and all that went on with such skill and precision.

But my energy came from a deeper place as well. It came from the joy of mastering new skills and being really useful and included in such important work. It came from my success. Barbara's mother told me I was a joy to have in the house.

Barbara had a little sister who was six years old. She drove the truck. It was her job to drive containers of water out to the field where the men were working. The first time I saw this, she was coming back from the field. I saw the truck coming slowly down the road, and I thought no one was driving it. Then I saw her little head peering out over the dashboard. I decided the farm was a magic place with rules all its own.

We didn't work all the time. I met many of Barbara's girl friends. I thought their life was exciting compared to Barbara's and my life at boarding school. But they thought ours was more exciting because we were away from home. I didn't tell them that at boarding school, I wasn't away from home. On Fridays, everyone piled into the trucks and went into town to a dance.

On Sundays, everyone dressed up and went into town to the Methodist church. They insisted on dropping me off at the Episcopal church on the way. The Episcopal church was a tiny building with a congregation consisting of about ten old people, me, and a seminarian who led the service. The seminarian was pretty cute, but he was all business. All the teenagers were at the large, overflowing Methodist church. I felt banished.

One Saturday afternoon, we went to a rodeo. We watched cowboys gallop horses around a dusty ring as they roped the cattle, swinging their ropes in intricate patterns. We teenagers sat in the bleachers eating hot dogs and drinking Cokes, not minding the hot sun beating down on our heads. Barbara's father stood right by the ring with a group of men wearing ten-gallon cowboy hats. I had never seen that many men together enjoying themselves. Barbara's father was in the legislature. Maybe they were talking politics. I think you would have enjoyed being there.

This month on the ranch was formative to my growing years, much as Blanche and the teachers at All Saints School were. I wish I could have told you about it right when it was happening.

All too soon, it was time for me to go back to school and for Barbara to go to college as she had graduated from All Saints School in June. My senior year began with a new room on the senior corridor. I now studied in my room in the evening because seniors didn't have to go to evening study hall. I also had a portable radio. Aunt Lida bought me a small radio for my birthday when we were in Portland, and at last I could use it.

As we moved into the familiar routine of the school year, I noticed a change in Mother. She was losing weight and neglecting her appearance. She wore a pair of my old, worn-out brown shoes that were a size too big for her. School staff and students wore white cotton uniforms for special chapel occasions, and she wore this uniform other times, such as when she worked in the office, even in the winter. With my old brown shoes, it gave her an even stranger appearance. Her hair grew long and straight, and she stopped going to the beauty parlor, explaining that it was too expensive and a waste of time. She had to have several teeth pulled and replaced by a removable bridge. But she didn't wear the bridge, and this resulted in a smile that was startling to say the least.

She got mad at me for reasons I didn't understand and refused to speak to me for several days. During these episodes, she refused to eat, complaining that her throat was closed, and she couldn't swallow. I left two candy bars in her room each day, and I noticed that every time, they had been eaten.

Sometimes, I still had those feelings of unreality when my eyes and brain felt disconnected. Seniors could go off campus without a chaperone, and, even though I loved this freedom, I had an attack of panic when I was downtown by myself. But I had learned to endure this and keep these fears of going insane strictly to myself.

School was going well, although I had history and civics classes from that teacher who thought I had an attitude problem. I had an attitude problem in chemistry too. But I was enrolled in a third year of French with Miss Dorland, a third year of math with Mrs. Close, and of course, Miss Dick's senior English class, which was wonderful.

As we know, I had come to appreciate boys during the time on the ranch. So when I was back at school, I couldn't help but notice that even sophomore and junior girls had boys calling them, coming to visit, and hanging around them after church. Some of the boys were getting taller, which made them even more attractive. But my dates continued to be "pair-ups" arranged for the dances.

I was included in a group of girls who were invited to model clothes for a charity fashion show at a downtown women's club. I modeled a white strapless formal that made me feel gorgeous. Several of the right ladies who were at the event told Mother how lovely I looked in the formal, so she bought it for me. When I wore it to the school dance, I had wild and wonderful fantasies about my future.

That year, our school play was *Little Women*. The production was arranged for an all-girls' school to perform, so it included a cast of only the women and girls—Marmee, the four daughters, Hannah the housekeeper, and Aunt March. Even with this limitation, it beautifully captured the essence of my beloved book. And I was chosen to play the part of Jo. The director, who was also that dreaded history teacher, had no way of knowing that Jo was my favorite character in my favorite book in the whole world. I became Jo as I hurled myself into the part in just the way I knew Jo would do it.

Friends of the school and from the town packed the auditorium for the performance.

My costume included a long hairpiece that just matched my own red hair. There is a scene in the story where Jo cuts off her hair and sells it so Marmee will have money to visit Father, who was wounded in the Civil War.

In this scene, I entered the stage without the hairpiece, put the money on Marmee's lap, and pulled off my hat to reveal the lost hair. Delores, the girl who played Marmee, was one of my good friends, and she played the role perfectly. I can still recite the dialogue between Marmee and Jo from memory.

There was not a dry eye in the house. At the end of the play, we took curtain calls and got rounds and rounds of applause, and the director told me to take one curtain call by myself. It was a moment of euphoria. Through Jo, I revealed myself—my longings, fear, and grief—and the audience connected with me. And as the cast mingled with the crowd for refreshments, one of the really popular boys smiled at me from across the room.

Soon it was time to make college plans. I had scored high in the college entrance examination all the seniors were required to take, and my grades continued to be very good. Uncle Raymond wrote to Mother suggesting that I apply to Whitman College, a very good liberal arts school that his son attended in southeastern Washington. He felt confident I would be accepted and perhaps qualify for scholarship aid. He said if finances should be a problem, he would be willing to help.

Of course, this is what I wanted to do, but it precipitated a crisis for Mother. She didn't know what to do with her life after I graduated. Her life had narrowed to her work at the school, her fascination with a supposed social status of Sioux Falls' Episcopalians, and a possession of me that seemed essential to her. What would happen to her if I went to Whitman? Miss Dorland began putting pressure on her to indicate the plans for both of us.

Mother simply couldn't visualize her next step. She decided not to let me go to Whitman. I was terribly disappointed but not surprised. I couldn't imagine that Mother's possessiveness would magically disappear when I graduated from high school. Finally, she agreed to let me enroll in the University of South Dakota. It was a hundred miles from Sioux Falls. I was accepted, she sent in the deposit, and my dorm room was assigned. She decided to find an apartment and stay in Sioux Falls. I thought this was going to work. Like the other three girls in my class, I was going away to college.

But it was not to happen. Out of the blue, Ed McKnight wrote and offered her a job as office manager in his food brokerage business in Seattle.

He said that he and Florence would find us an apartment. I could live with Mother and go to the University of Washington. She accepted his offer immediately. My fate was sealed for the next four years.

All too soon, it was high school graduation day. Blanche and Freddy came from Minneapolis for the occasion. They also came to say good-bye to us. We were going much further away, which meant visits would be even more infrequent. I remember little about the ceremony or the baccalaureate the day before. I do remember saying good-bye to my friends and teachers, including the history teacher who cast me in the play. The 'bishop's pet" bishop gave me a card with a handwritten note inside.

Everyone left, but Mother and I stayed one more night. I walked the empty corridors and halls, to the library, classrooms, dining room, and the chapel, feeling like I was letting go of a life that I had outgrown. The next day, Miss Dorland drove us to the train. As the train pulled away, I saw her waving from the platform, but I couldn't cry. We were off to a new life in Seattle.

Chapter 11

It was the Seattle where you, Dad, marched down Second Avenue with your regiment on your way to France in the First World War. (I am noticing that, at last, I am thinking of you as Dad. I love to write those words.) It was the Seattle where you began your work at J. A. Campbell Company and the Seattle where you and Mother met. For me, at the threshold of the University of Washington in 1951, this seemed like ancient history.

Our small apartment was a mile north of the University. It was on the ground floor of a small apartment building. The front door opened directly to the outside where small flowering shrubs and trees bedecked a tiny yard; the first home of our own that I could remember.

Mother shipped furniture from Minneapolis where it had ended up after the Portland years. Blanche had befriended it and kept it all this time. It included that French provincial cherrywood desk you had given Mother, as well as your large comfortable chair that I remembered as Freddy's special chair in their Minneapolis home. Mother had the chair recovered and placed it by the front living room window. As I sat in it and looked up from whatever book I happened to be reading, I could gaze out on our small front yard.

Your bedroom furniture arrived. Our apartment had one bedroom, and, of course, that furniture included a double bed. Mother's plan was that we were to sleep together. I refused to get in that bed with her, so each night I made up a bed on the living room couch. After a month of this, when I still wouldn't budge from my stance, she finally sold the double bed and bought twin beds.

In addition to this furniture from your early life, Mother bought a couch, tables, chairs, lamps, dishes, pots and pans, cooking utensils, and a coffee pot. I had a hard time believing that everything really belonged to us.

Despite the disappointment over not going away to college, I was struck with the feeling that I belonged in Seattle and felt that the West Coast was my real home. This was strange because I hardly remembered the years I lived in Portland, and I had spent fourteen of my growing-up years in the Midwest. The Pacific Northwest embraced me.

I loved the mountains and the water. I jumped into Puget Sound and tasted salt water for the first time. I actually almost convinced myself that Elliott Bay had been named after us. I even loved the rain, and I appreciated the cooler air without oppressive humidity and the warmer winter where ice and snow were such rare novelties that they closed the University when the snow depth reached beyond one inch. My palate discovered crab, shrimp, and salmon, and eating in a restaurant became a delight.

Of course, the Elliott family was very glad to have us back in their turf. Aunt Agnes and Uncle Charles still lived in Seattle. I remember that there was a time when you stayed with them during your bachelor days after the war. Aunt Agnes, the oldest in the family—small, yet indomitable—was short and plump with curly gray hair framing her determined-looking face. Didn't she have a long-standing reputation for being bossy and demanding? Tall, white-haired Uncle Charles was a quiet man and very deaf by then. This might have been to his advantage. He seemed to go along with all of his wife's ideas or plans.

Almost immediately, Aunt Lida came up on the train for a visit. Uncle Earl had heart trouble, and his health was failing quickly, but Aunt Lida made the trip all the same. Uncle Raymond and Aunt Gertrude came from Pendleton to see us shortly afterward.

Soon, Uncle Earl died. Mother insisted that she was too busy at work to go to Portland for the funeral, but I was to go anyway. I protested wildly. I had never been to a funeral and was afraid to go without her.

"Can't we both stay home?" I cried in anguish. "We can send a sympathy card. I'll write a note on it."

But she insisted that I go. I rode to Portland with Aunt Agnes and Uncle Charles, and Mother stayed home from work until she saw that I had actually gotten in the car. I put on my most grown-up face on the journey to Portland, but I was terrified because I knew deep inside, despite my bravado, I was not grown up enough for this funeral.

The funeral was the Elliott family at its very best. Aunt Lida's small home was packed with people both before and after the service. Some of them I knew, some I thought maybe I knew, and some just melted into a blur of kind folks who seemed to know me but I didn't know at all.

When we went to the funeral home for the service, Aunt Gertrude immediately took charge of me in her quiet way. At the end of the service, the casket was opened, and everyone was to file by to look at Uncle Earl for one last time. Although her own college-aged children were there needing her support as well, she took my arm and spoke reassuringly to me as we took our place in line and walked lovingly by the casket.

"It doesn't look like Uncle Earl at all," she murmured softly. I will always remember Aunt Gertrude helping me through my first funeral. Was she thinking of walking past your open casket sixteen years before? I wonder who had been there to help her.

After the funeral, food appeared by magic as we returned to Aunt Lida's home. The other young people escaped outside, eager to put some distance between themselves and this smothering hoard of grieving relatives. But I stayed in the house in the midst of the smothering, knowing that right then it was where I belonged.

The University of Washington's buildings sprawled over acres and acres of campus. I, who had come from a high school of 25 girls, found myself one of 12,000 students, a bewildering array of age and variety. My classes were large, and the professors seemed demanding and impersonal. For the first time, I struggled with school, and I felt humiliated. My grades plummeted, and I was ashamed to tell anyone about my struggles.

I was also ashamed to tell anyone about the small boarding school, my difficult mother, my dead father, my feelings of disconnection and unreality, and my fear that I might go insane. I felt different. I had my secrets. Everyone else seemed to have come from homes and families and large, coeducational high schools.

It was taken for granted in Sioux Falls that I would pledge a sorority, and the social status of this appealed to Mother, but only if I continued to live in the apartment with her. Of course, I pushed for living a mile away in a sorority and leaving her in the apartment to keep a place for me to come home for vacations. Finally, I declined the invitation to go through rush. I knew that she would be threatened by the centrality the sorority would require in my life. She would have embarrassing and frightening fits if I needed to be there, and she wanted to be included or to have me with her. She seemed addicted to the control she had over my life and refused to see any other way we might live. Now I had another secret. I pretended that I didn't approve of sororities, that I was too good for them. I let on, and almost convinced myself, that living in the apartment with my mother was a superior way of being.

I soon made connection with Canterbury Club, the Episcopal student organization at Christ Episcopal Church not far from campus. Christ Church became my church home and Canterbury became my central college community. I wanted Mother to join me on Sundays for church, but she refused, explaining that she was too busy. Some of the church members invited college students to their homes, and I soon came to know many of them.

Canterbury life, administered by a college chaplain and a young woman who was a director of Christian education, included Sunday evening programs with speakers and discussion groups, a Thursday noon lunch, and social time provided by the church ladies as well as dances, social events, and just general "hanging out" in the Canterbury lounge.

Boys soon discovered me. They weren't called boys anymore. They were taller than my five feet eight inches and were referred to as men. Many even drove cars. I was astonished at my popularity and sex appeal. The school uniform was long behind me, and I wore sweaters and skirts in styles and colors that showed off my long legs, slender curves, and the red hair I was coming to appreciate. I remember my freshman year in Canterbury as raging hormones with a religious overlay.

Yes, I know this shocks you. You needed to be alive and in my life to worry about me as fathers do when young men begin noticing their daughters. I needed you, I needed Mother, I needed Blanche, and I needed Mrs. Close. I longed for someone to be with me in this guilty struggle to understand my new passions and behaviors. But in these new struggles with growing up, would I have kept secrets from all of you as well?

The age of the Canterbury members ranged from freshmen through graduate students. There were some people who had already graduated, and Christ Church attracted young single people wanting a place to connect with others. Some of the men were headed for Episcopal seminary. This hodgepodge of diverse types and ages reminded me of my life in boarding houses when I was a child. I was welcomed and belonged and made good friends. It was a place where I was taken at face value. I didn't have to explain what my life was like before college. In my insecurity, my secrets were safe.

As I think about Canterbury now, I reflect on the richness of diversity we took for granted in this group. One person, already a painter, went on to be an accomplished artist. An exchange student from Nigeria became its vice president. There was a history professor in the making. There were all types of engineering, education, and political science majors.

An architecture major became an architect in American Samoa. Some men went on to seminary to become priests. Most of us, sooner or later, became husbands, wives, and parents, and many are still active lay people in Episcopal churches. The director of religious education went on to marry a priest and scholar, and they spent considerable time in Israel and Southwest Africa, living and writing about the challenges of diversity in those countries in the 1960s.

Born during the great depression of the 1930s, I was the first generation on either side of the family to go to college. Many parents saw a college education as a ticket to a higher social class and to opportunities for better paying professional jobs. I wonder if this contributed to Mother's obsession with those "right people." Like Uncle Raymond and Aunt Gertrude as well as Blanche and Freddy, you all were hardworking and self-taught, focused on jobs, homes, families, and your local communities. You took pride when you planned to save money to make college possible for your children. I know Mother insisted on this. We both knew how much you would have wanted it. But I soon found college much more than a shoo-in to the upper middle class.

Suddenly, I was awash in liberal politics, international awareness, and social action. From both sides of my family, I had known nothing but Republicans. You and Mother both came from small towns that were farming-centered communities that took pride in being mainly Republican. Uncle Raymond and Uncle Freddy were both hardworking Republican businessmen.

This was also true of my boarding school environment. If I thought of this at all as I grew up, I thought that all Episcopalians were Republicans—Mother's mysterious "right kind of people." Since history and civics had not been my strong subjects in high school—and since I had never even knowingly met a Democrat—this was an expansion of my awareness, and it was dizzying in magnitude. I quickly found out that Episcopalians sometimes were Democrats.

The University was liberal in its orientation. This was a time of great fear of Communism in the United States. Joseph McCarthy, a fanatical Republican senator, headed a national committee requiring college professors who were suspected of being Communists, despite inconclusive and questionable evidence, to sign loyalty oaths. A number of University of Washington professors were being threatened with the destruction of their careers and possible imprisonment if they did not do this. Among them was my English literature professor, who refused to sign the loyalty oath out of principle, and as a result, he feared for his future.

My Republican background became another of my secrets. It would be a number of years before I could clearly explain and defend it. This demand to experience and understand a larger, complex world when I had yet to understand my own world sometimes left me angry and frightened. In retrospect, I am glad my college life didn't center on a sorority, one of the last bastions of Republicanism on campus. At Canterbury, I began to listen, learn, and think for myself.

The other organization that was formative in these college years was the University YM/YWCA. Here, I met foreign students from all over the world.

There was social and community outreach and an awareness of a larger world in the programs. World War II was in the past, and I learned about a new organization, the United Nations. It consisted of representatives from nearly every nation cooperating to maintain international security and peace by fair negotiation. I was deeply moved by these discussions and convictions.

Each year, we sponsored an International Ball in the Student Union Building. Seeing students from different races dancing together was exhilarating. In the summer, we spent a week at a nearby conference center. In addition to speakers and discussions, we enjoyed the outdoors together, swimming, hiking, and what seemed like an eternal game of volleyball. Every evening, we folk danced, and students from all over the world taught and shared their dances.

I remember Margaret Norton, an Episcopalian who was the YWCA director. I thrived under Margaret's leadership. Her pleasant face, framed with soft, prematurely gray curls, seemed present to every moment. She knew the best ways to challenge each girl toward personal development combined with a greater awareness of the world's challenges. She reminded me of Miss Dorland in the ways she approached her job. But unlike Miss Dorland, Margaret was divorced, a single mother with a teenage daughter. She smoked, and we called her by her first name. She was a wise and special friend. Margaret spoke personally about her own issues, specifically about being divorced and raising a daughter. My life with Mother was not at all like hers. I was ashamed, and I kept my secret.

I carried into my adult life an appreciation of this kind of woman: single and well educated, with an autonomy I admire but could never completely emulate. I always try to keep one or two of this type of women in my life.

An embarrassing secret I could not keep was my struggle in the physical education classes required for freshmen and sophomores. Every incoming freshman was required to pass a swimming test. I didn't pass, so I had to take the beginning swimming class. Soon I was swimming the length of the pool and treading water for five minutes. These were the requirements for graduation. The next quarter I liked swimming so much that I registered for the intermediate class. I did fine until the final examination came at the end of the quarter. I panicked when I was required to walk out on the diving board and jump off, even though the diving board was only four feet above the water.

"You won't graduate unless you jump off that board," the instructor shouted at me in desperation.

"Then I won't graduate," I retorted and walked into the locker room. For four years, this worry remained on my mind, but I graduated with no further mention of my deficiency. You would have taught me to swim and dive early in my life as Uncle Raymond enjoyed doing with his children. I know you feel sad about this.

We also might have gone skiing. I registered for beginning skiing because it sounded exciting, and the mountains and local enthusiasm for skiing captivated my imagination. It was also captivated by the idea of riding the ski bus with some very attractive boys. But I twisted my knee on the ski tow the second week, and I had to drop the class.

Finally, my advisor encouraged me to register for bowling and a basic P.E. class consisting mostly of calisthenics. This satisfied P.E. requirements with assured success.

Although I made a joke of this and let on that P.E. wasn't important, I really felt that it was. I wanted my body to enjoy it; I wanted to gain skills and do well. I was secretly humiliated by being less capable than most of the other girls.

The winter I was a freshman, I found myself seriously over my head in a trigonometry class. My advisor recommended the class because I had done so well in high school math. But I soon learned that the reality of college math made it much different from Mrs. Close's encouraging ways. The class was full of ROTC men who seemed to understand everything before it was even presented. I was the only girl in the class, and the professor, a short, thin man with skimpy hair and a hawklike nose, instantly looked on me with suspicion.

To top it off, one day in my nervousness, I was fiddling with my pearl necklace. Suddenly it broke, spilling the pearls across what seemed to be every inch of floor in the room. Students hit the floor in every direction, crawling around and retrieving the pearls, as the professor stood helplessly at the blackboard, chalk in hand, his class gone from his grasp. I was in serious trouble, and I needed to pass this class.

Art, one of the young men in Canterbury, volunteered to help me. A junior classman, Art was tall, blond, and slender with blue eyes that reflected his tendency to be shy. Art loved math and was very good at trigonometry. He talked me through each homework assignment. I passed the class with a C and acquired a new friend in the process.

Art was a mountain climber. That spring, he was climbing Mount St. Helens with a group of mountaineers. He fell into a crevasse, and, following a long, unsuccessful effort of the mountain rescue team to bring him up alive, he died a slow, agonizing death still trapped in the crevasse.

When word came over the radio of Art's fall and the rescue efforts already in place, Canterbury students gathered in the church basement, needing to be together to await news of his rescue. When the news came that Art had died, the grief-stricken chaplain left the church immediately without further word. Finally, we all quietly dispersed, almost as if it were an ordinary day. Although many of us attended the funeral a few days later, we talked very little about his death in the days to come. Episcopalians were reserved and dignified about public expression of grief. We students ran the risk of being labeled "immature" or "not brave enough" or "lacking in right theology" or, in the case of the girls, "hysterical." After a while, Art's tragic death was treated like something that had happened a long time ago, and the community should be over it by now.

Art's brother, Fred, came to the University and to Canterbury that following fall. Two years younger than Art, Fred was slender and not quite as tall. His eyes were darker, and he sported a very short, signature crew cut. Although I didn't know Art's family, I had written them a note of condolence at the time of his death telling them about the time Art spent with me helping me through trigonometry. Fred remembered that I had ended the note with the words, "You must be wonderful parents to have such a fine son."

Fred soon sought me out, and we spent hours together while he poured out his grief. His pain, loneliness, and helpless anguish gushed from inside of him in torrents of words.

As I listened to Fred's story, this pouring out of raw grief, I came to know that I could listen like this. To begin with, there was no one else for him to talk to. Then there was my secret—the secret that I, too, was acquainted with grief.

There was the grief for you and for my infant home, and yes, grief for Mother who became less and less accessible at every turn. Surely, God was with both Fred and me at that time.

There is a scene in the opera *Hansel and Gretel* that touches deeply my memories of that time. Hansel and Gretel are lost in the woods and night is falling. Gretel says, "Come, Hansel, we must pray."

As darkness continues to fall, they join hands and sing with gorgeous music and a full chorus that beautiful aria, "When in deep distress I stand, God the Father takes my hand."

Then fourteen beautiful angels slowly and gracefully descend from heaven and surround them as the darkness envelops the stage. Although we were nineteen years old, spiritually, Fred and I were parentless children lost in the woods with night falling. Angels must have surrounded us.

I soon met Fred's mother. She was a teacher, and she invited me to visit her school as I was thinking about becoming a teacher. When we sat eating lunch alone in her classroom, suddenly she began to weep and talk of her own heart-wrenching suffering as she went over in her mind and soul the day the accident happened. She also needed someone to talk to. I managed to offer a listening presence.

I think my strength came from several places. First, knowing Mother's grief from way back in my preverbal, earliest beginnings. Second, living with Mrs. H's helpless anger in the face of her husband's alcoholism, and third, experiencing Blanche's grief at the time of her hysterectomy. Finally, I remembered Aunt Lida telling me about her wrenching loss when you died. And it came from my own secret, buried grief for you, still deep inside me. From a very early age, I was destined to be a listener.

Fred went on to become an Episcopal priest. For a number of years, he was a missionary priest on the Rosebud Indian reservation in South Dakota. In churches he serves, he is acutely sensitive as he ministers to those who may be grieving. Many years later, I was instrumental in developing a pastoral care program for my church. This college time was formative for both of us. We both became writers. We remain close friends today.

Chapter 12

Mother complained about how hard she worked at Marsh and Company, Ed McKnight's food brokerage business. The regular workweek of forty hours usually expanded to an extra hour on weekdays. In addition, she went to the office on many Saturdays. She didn't like to take the city bus to work, so Ed would swing by the apartment and pick her up on his way to work. Usually, she would stay late enough that he would drive her home as well. He said that it was on his way and was no trouble for him. He had a luxury car, and Mother enjoyed the service and the comfort.

Although she often complained that she was overworked and not appreciated, she enjoyed the atmosphere of the business. Business associates from out of town regularly came to the office for meetings with Ed, and she came to know them. They appreciated her familiar presence and her conscientious work. Perhaps they reminded her of you and your life together and her dream of what you might have become if you had not died.

However, Jack, one of the McKnight's sons, managed the Portland branch of the business. Florence did not like Jack's wife and, as a result, refused to speak to Jack or have anything to do with him or his wife. Ed took Mother with him on one of his trips to the Portland office. Jack and his wife invited both of them to dinner at their home. When Florence heard about this, she was furious. She refused to have us in her home after that and never spoke to Mother again. This severed her connection with the memories and a former way of life that had brought us back to Seattle. Mother rarely spoke of this ruptured friendship and continued to work at Marsh and Company until it dissolved eight year later when Ed retired. Except for me, it was the only thing she had in her life.

By the time I was a junior, my academic life settled down. Classes became easier or perhaps my concentration became better. I declared a major in elementary education that provided a vocational focus for me. I knew that as soon as I finished school and had a teaching job, I could leave Mother.

I also had a part-time student job in the admissions office of the University, gaining experience in the working world while making some extra money as well. I lived on hope. In addition to the Y and Canterbury communities, I hung out with others taking education classes. I had a best friend in Canterbury, Betty. Betty also lived at home with a single mother, and I absorbed some of her mother's good nurturing ways when I spent time there.

Betty was a year ahead of me in school and married Don, another member of Canterbury, right after her graduation. I was the maid of honor in the wedding. The next spring, they had a baby boy, and I became a godmother. Fred continued to be important in my life as did Don's brother Ted, a seminary student who went off to New York each school year, but he swept me off my feet when he came home for vacations. Late in my junior year, I also began dating Bill, a young Boeing engineer—one of the post-college types who hung out at Canterbury.

As a senior, I did an academic quarter of practice teaching in the first grade of a public school. I was assigned to a school in an inner city that was in an interracial part of Seattle. Mother was furious. She wanted me at one of the schools in an upper middle class neighborhood.

"You asked for this with your do-gooder ways." She spit out these words with a vengeance that surprised even me. She would sometimes refer to what she described as my "do-gooder ways" when I spoke of social outreach or empathy for someone who was poor, but I didn't expect it in reference to a school assignment.

I loved the children and all I was teaching and learning. The school was what we used to describe as a melting pot of races. However, I acquired another secret. I saw that the pot wasn't really melting. One day, the principal, a white educator who was well known and respected in the school district, burst into our classroom with a wooden paddle. He brought a little black boy named Isaac to the front of the classroom and hit his bottom hard with the paddle because the teacher reported that he had misbehaved. I can still see this small, slender first-grader and hear his shrieks of helpless pain and humiliation. The paddle was larger than his little bottom.

After the principal left, the teacher lined up the children to go out for recess. When her back was turned, the little boys looked at each other and giggled, playfully pretending to spank one another, including Isaac in this horseplay. Isaac began to giggle, and the tears dried on his face as they filed out to the playground.

I said nothing to anyone about this, knowing it would cause trouble I was not prepared to handle. Although I was overcome with guilt, my "do-gooder ways" were no match for this incident. It became another of my secrets.

As I tell our story, I reflect on how often I talk about what I describe as my secrets. In these university years, these secrets were in my inability to talk to those around me about your death and my growing up with Mother in such bizarre ways, smothered in her anger and fear. They were also the secrets I kept from Mother—the expansion of my awareness and experience from the constrained ways she imagined for me.

Then there were my continuing fears of going insane, my terrors, the feelings of unreality that still came over me during those times of panic and phobia. Deep within myself, I walked an emotional tightrope. My experience of living on this tightrope was the best-kept secret of all, that sense of the presence of God and glimmers of your continuing influence coming from Uncle Raymond and the Elliott family. I lived a protected life of inner solitude.

Chapter 13

I graduated from college in the summer of 1955 with a job and an escape plan. I left Mother and moved to Puyallup, a small town thirty miles south of Seattle where I was hired to teach first grade. I moved into an apartment with two other newly minted teachers, Connie and Helen.

Connie was a talented art teacher. With a neat cap of brown hair framing a quiet, thoughtful face, she was reserved in a manner that tended to perfectionism. Helen was a Spanish teacher. Her boyfriend was a Frenchman. Helen's brown eyes sparkled with intensity whenever she spoke, which was nearly all the time. Helen never told a short story when a long story was possible.

The sprawling apartment was an entire second floor of an old home in the original section of Puyallup. It was very near railroad tracks that bisected the town, and we got used to sleeping through the sound of trains barreling through at odd hours. The owners lived downstairs and rented to teachers because we were thought to be respectable and reliable tenants. The apartment was furnished with odds and ends of hand-me-down furniture. We collected some kitchenware, sheets, and towels; put a plant in the kitchen window; and a fat candle on the living room coffee table, and we were home.

All of a sudden, I was responsible for the education of twenty-five first graders. I jumped right in and pretended I knew what I was doing. The teaching staff was made up of very seasoned teachers along with a sprinkling of us neophytes. The principal was understanding and helpful, and the superintendent of this small school district treated all of the teachers like we were his family. Many of the parents had grown up in Puyallup or surrounding areas, and they respected the teachers as important people in the community.

In their eyes, the teacher was always right, even the twenty-two-year-olds. Although my experience was nonexistent, every child I taught was a special gift, and I look back on this community of teachers and parents as formative during this year when I finished growing up.

I was making my own money. Every month there was a paycheck. With all three of us budgeting carefully and sharing expenses, I was slowly developing a bank account.

Right away, friends from college found out where we lived and made regular trips to Puyallup to visit us. Connie and Helen both were going steady with serious boyfriends. It was not respectable for teachers to be seen buying alcoholic beverages, so the guys, Pierre and Scott, picked up beer and wine for us.

On Friday nights, the boys usually showed up. We lit the candle on the coffee table, put records on Connie's high fidelity record player, and sat around on the floor drinking beer, using licorice sticks as straws.

Bill, that young Boeing engineer from Canterbury, regularly made the trip to Puyallup, and as the year moved on, he became increasingly central in our social schema, always bringing a share of the beer and wine. His inclusion was not without its struggles.

Connie often made beautiful seasonal decorations for the apartment. At Christmastime, she filled a huge brandy snifter with whole nuts mixed with small, multicolored Christmas tree balls. She centered a candle in the middle of this arrangement, lit the candle, and put it on our coffee table for a Friday evening gathering. As the evening wore on, Bill began to eat the nuts from the snifter. The candle began to tilt, but Bill continued to eat the nuts, cracking them in his hand. Much to everyone else's amusement, Connie began to scowl and sent more and more angry looks Bill's way. As the evening wore on, the nuts continued to diminish, and the candle tilted at a forty-five degree angle.

"That boyfriend of yours—I can't believe what he did," Connie howled after everyone had gone. I laughed indulgently. Cutting through the artistic, Bill had gone right for the food. This was a flesh-and-blood man. I thought he was wonderful.

Helen, also laughing, defended him. "It's not like he ate the Christmas tree balls," she observed, but Connie was not comforted.

In March, Helen and Pierre married and moved into a nearby apartment. They still showed up on Friday nights. Connie became resigned to the fact that Bill continued to show up as well. Bill became more and more central in my life. We became engaged in April and were married on July 21, 1956.

Chapter 14

"You got married? Who is this man?" I can almost hear you gasp and say these words. How I wish you had been right there, giving him the once over, this Bill, tall with brown eyes and tousled brown hair. He looks very Welsh, characteristic of the ancestry on his father's side. Oh yes, our last name is Lloyd. Janet Elliott was gone forever. I became Janet Lloyd. How I wish that you and Bill could have known each other.

Bill grew up in Rockville Centre, New York, on Long Island, and went to college at Worcester Polytechnic Institute in Massachusetts. Like me, he was an only child, born after his parents had been married and childless for many years His parents adored him to the point of centering their marriage around him but were dominating and possessive in the extreme. In both parents' extended families, alienation from one another accelerated to the degree that they were not speaking. Although Bill's parents had a few close family friends, and his mother was involved in clubs and social activities, Bill grew up in a confusing, controlling adult world.

Unlike me, Bill lived in the same house on a tree-lined street until he went to college. His father went by commuter train into the city to work each day and was home for dinner every night. Bill managed to skip a grade and a half as he went through school and graduated from high school when he was sixteen and from college when he was twenty. He, who had never been east of New York City, arrived in Seattle to work as an electrical engineer at Boeing five months before his twenty-first birthday. Because he was an Episcopalian, he found Christ Church and Canterbury Club very soon. He is a wonderful singer, and the first time I remember noticing him was as he processed down the aisle in the church choir.

When you first held me in your arms, did you dream of the day you would walk me down the aisle on my wedding day? Even though I didn't remember you, I missed you so very much. There was an empty place in my heart, and I knew it was where you were supposed to be. Before the service, I put a special vase of flowers on the church altar in your memory.

Most of the Elliott family came for the wedding. Uncle Raymond served as your representative, walking me proudly down the aisle as he gave me away in traditional fashion. Aunt Mae's Seattle granddaughter was a junior bridesmaid.

The college chaplain married us in Christ Church—still our church home. With college friends, Canterbury friends, and the Elliott family, the church was nearly full of well-wishers who were caught up in the excitement of the occasion.

Bill's parents flew to Seattle for the wedding.

"Haven't you made him quit smoking yet?" These were Bill's mother's first words of greeting when Bill and I met them at the airport. Bill's father, quiet and nervous, with quick, rabbit-like motions, managed to collect the baggage as he proudly showed us the champagne glasses he had snuck in his pocket from the airplane.

"The airplane was boring!" Bill's mother dismissed the adventure of her first flight. "Nothing to see out the window but clouds."

"Be sure to put paper on the seat," She called to me from the adjoining stall as we stopped in the ladies room. We weren't even out of the airport yet.

"Is it always hot in Seattle?" She went on to complain as we walked to the car.

Bill and his father walked ahead with the suitcases, leaving us trailing along behind. I soon learned that Bill's father was accommodating in the extreme. Like Bill, he was quiet. Bill's mother talked every waking moment and assaulted me with her words. I could see immediately that I was a threat. I was caught in a vise of criticism and control.

"How is your mother doing with this wedding?" I know you're wondering about that. With only three months' notice, she soon became resigned to its reality. I think she knew inside herself that I would inevitably marry, and she wouldn't be successful in interfering. She approved of the idea that Bill was through college and had a job in Seattle. He didn't plan to take me away. I know she had terror that I would marry one of those young men going away to the military or to graduate school in Europe or to seminary in New York.

Bill and I had the independence and authority of our own money. We both had good jobs and paid for much of the wedding.

"I can never find a dress," Mother insisted. "Nothing will fit me." Finally, I bought a lovely blue dress and hat and gave them to her. They fit perfectly. She went to the beauty parlor and had her hair done and looked lovely.

I treasure a memory of the morning of the wedding. She and I sat in her living room, each putting on nail polish. I felt a quiet, companionable peace and a connection palpable in its intensity. Somehow, we managed not to spoil the moment with words. There was nothing we could say.

Finally, Bill and I were off for a two-week honeymoon; we were married people, guilt-free, away from the stress and complexity of parents. I had a beautiful white satin nightgown. In this early time of our marriage, Bill took the nightgown off me as we lay in bed. The he gently put it back on, only to take it off again. "It's like unwrapping a present," he explained. "I want to wrap it up and unwrap it over and over again."

The first week was a honeymoon. We drove down the Oregon coast just enjoying each other. The second week was vacation. We went over to central Oregon, and Bill was immersed in the Elliott family. We stayed with Uncle George and Aunt Bertha. Bill was sunburned by then from our time at the ocean. I was peeling long strips of dead skin from his back.

"They have only been married for a week, and she is already skinning him alive," Uncle George teased.

As sunburned as he was, Bill loved the farm. He went everywhere with Uncle George and his son Fred, learning all about farming and the realities of irrigation in that region. We hiked, experiencing the hot dry country. We learned to ride horses from Uncle George's son Sid. We saw mountains in the distance bordering the hot dry terrain: Mount Jefferson, Broken Top, and the Three Sisters. Uncle George relayed the local legend explaining Broken Top's unusual shape. Broken Top had insulted one of the three sisters, so Jefferson knocked his top off.

Of course, all the family that lived there gathered for a picnic at Aunt Mae and Uncle Bill's, the original family home. I know your presence was felt, and you were deeply thought of by everyone as they enjoyed our visit.

"When you have your first baby, I'll come and be with you," insisted Aunt Nina. She was the one in the family that always helped the new mothers. Her invitation proved life-giving to me in the time to come. As we returned from our honeymoon, Bill knew that my Elliott family was his family as well.

Then it was September and school began. So I could keep my job, we decided to live in Puyallup, and Bill would commute to his job at Boeing, a forty-five minute drive each way. We moved to a brand-new duplex apartment. Our landlords, Mr. and Mrs. Martin, lived next door in a very old, big house with a wraparound front porch. Landlords they were in the classic sense of the word. The house originally belonged to his parents, who were early settlers in Puyallup. They built the duplex on the site of an old barn on the original property. They were grandparent types, friendly, caring, and nurturing toward their tenants. They had married children and grandchildren who visited often, generating much activity. The property backed up to the high school athletic field, and on fall evenings, we could watch football games through the fence. Mrs. Martin taught me to bake bread and make pies.

Helen and Pierre had moved to San Francisco, but Connie and Scott lived in Puyallup. They often came for beer and licorice sticks on Friday evening. Sometimes I made spaghetti and garlic bread as well.

Bill got to know many of the teachers, including two young men who lived in the other half of the duplex. We frequently gathered for picnics and parties.

Bill and I often went back to Seattle and Christ Church on Sundays, and then we went to Mother's apartment for dinner.

I was in raptures of delight as we shopped for furniture. We bought a dark mahogany four-poster bed that was elegant to behold. I proudly covered it with a beautiful silk comforter that was a wedding present. We went to bed feeling like the lord and lady of a grand manor. But this new furniture could be traumatic.

Bill's old alarm clock sat on the nightstand. He was very attached to this clock because it had been his companion all through college. By this time, pieces of masking tape wound around it kept it together. Without warning, it had a way of setting off a loud, sustained buzzing sound in the middle of the night. The only way the sound could be stopped was by sharply hitting the top of the clock.

In these early months of marriage, we both had trouble sleeping.

"Janet Elliott? Oh my God, what is she doing here?" Bill would rouse in the night and look beside him, momentarily disoriented. Often I would toss and turn, not yet comfortable with sleeping with Bill. And as beautiful as it was, that comforter always slid around, ending up on the floor. One of us was always scrambling for it in the cold darkness.

In the middle of the night, the clock began buzzing. Bill reached over me to hit it, and the bed fell down. This happened several nights before Bill realized the slats holding up the box spring were too short. He confided the problem to Mr. Martin, who invited him into his workshop to make longer slats. I'm sure Mr. and Mrs. Martin privately chuckled about our mishap.

On one of the Sunday visits, we told Mother about the difficulties with the bed slats, comforter, and clock. Naturally, we didn't tell her about Bill's occasional night terrors. She must have told Blanche about this in a letter because Blanche sent us a blanket and a clock for Christmas.

Bill hated throwing out his old clock. It was my first glimpse of how much he resists change. I folded the comforter, and put it on a shelf where it stayed for years before I gave it to Goodwill.

By November 1956, I knew I was pregnant. We had planned that I would quit teaching at the end of that school year, move to Seattle, buy a house, and then have a baby. It would be a boy, William Marklove Lloyd III. Bill insisted he would be named after him and his father. But Mark, as we would call him for short, had other plans. He was to be born in July.

We didn't tell anyone the news until January. It was hard not saying anything, particularly at Thanksgiving when we took Mother to central Oregon with us for the annual Elliott gathering. Each year, Elliotts from far and wide traveled to the Madras Grange Hall for a huge Thanksgiving dinner.

"Remember, you promised to come when we have our first baby," I winked as I managed to whisper to Aunt Nina as we were leaving for home.

We spent our first married Christmas keeping our secret. This was partly because we wanted to wait as long as possible to tell my school principal. We hoped I would be allowed to teach the rest of the year. We needed the money if we were to buy a house. The second reason, although perhaps unconscious, was how Mother would react when we told her. All too soon, we found out.

"Janet, how could you?" She turned pale as she spat out the words. For a moment, she stood wringing her hands, a look of despair on her face. Then she ran to the bathroom, and we could hear her throwing up. "You will be fat and ugly—as big as a house," she finally came out of the bathroom and took up where she left off. "Believe me, you will never be the same. Your life is over when you have a baby."

I should have known she would react this way, but still, my mind reeled with shock. How could she treat me this way when I needed her so much? But that's how it was.

My principal said I could teach as long as I felt able to continue the job. I did manage to finish the school year with a full salary for the year.

This first year of marriage brought the reality that I had never before lived with a man sharply into focus. I had not experienced a toilet seat always up, size thirteen shoes tripping me when I walked across the bedroom floor in the dark, the smell of a clothes hamper full of dirty socks and Jockey underwear, fish heads in the sink after Bill's fishing excursions, or an opera singer's aria full volume on Bill's high fidelity record player as she spent fifteen minutes dying, the sound reverberating against bare walls and floors.

Then there were Bill's migraine headaches, I knew Bill suffered with these, but I didn't fully comprehend how badly he suffered until that first year of our marriage.

About every four months, he had a series of headaches occurring as often as every other day. A series would last about three weeks. First flashes of light exploded in one of his eyes. Then agonizing pain began on one side of his face. The pain reached a crescendo in three or four hours then gradually tapered off, leaving him spent and exhausted. During these headaches, a spasm of blood vessels on his face looked like clusters of tiny grapes under his skin. Often, he threw up during a migraine attack.

What sometimes helped was placing alternating hot and very cold, wrung-out washcloths on the affected side of his face. Reheating, recooling, and reapplying the washcloths were jobs I could do. Bill remembers that these headaches began when he was sixteen. They miraculously and mysteriously disappeared when he was thirty-seven.

In these ways, the first married year moved on. My energy held up at school. It held up at home as well. I temporarily eliminated beer and licorice sticks from my diet.

In March, we drove to Seattle on weekends to look for a house, and soon our new home was in the making. We found a brand-new development in Bellevue, a suburb east of Seattle across Lake Washington by way of a newly constructed floating bridge. Its delightful name was Robinswood. We tramped through mud, choosing the best lot available for us. In the real estate office, which was the garage in the model home, we chose one of several possible house plans along with paint colors, carpeting, and appliances. It would be ready in September when the baby would be two months old. The lot was toward the top of a hilly street. There was a view of a small lake with the Cascade Mountains in the distance. Nearly every weekend, we drove to Bellevue to see how the house was coming along,

"Did you still feel you would go insane?" I know you are asking. "Did you have panic attacks, that terrible feeling of disconnection?"

Bill became my safe person. No matter the panic or the disconnection, oddly, I knew I wouldn't go insane. I would survive because Bill was there, although I never talked to anyone about these episodes until years later.

Just as I had never lived with a man, Bill had not lived with a woman for any length of time since he was sixteen. He assumed that any climate of anxiety or fear I generated was simply the nature of a woman when you really got to know her. At the same time, I was Bill's safe person when he had his headaches. He knew I needed him. I would stay with him as he exposed the indescribable agony of the headaches.

I finished the school year on June 3, more than ready for my expanding body not to be moving at the speed and contortions of twenty-five first-graders. The teachers had a baby shower for me, and I began to get clothes and equipment ready for the pending arrival.

"Who helped you?" I can hear your cry of love, despair, and concern. "Who was a mother for you? Where was your family?"

First, there was Mrs. Martin. During those five weeks between the end of school and Mark's birth, we would sit in rocking chairs on her porch several times a week talking about babies. She told me of her childbirth experiences and about her life when she was a new mother. She told me about the births of her grandchildren and how their mothers managed. "What wonderful parents I know you and Bill will be." She said this so many times as we rocked together on that porch. She reminded me of the way Mrs. Close talked to me about college in my high school years.

Then there was my cousin Genevieve. She is Aunt Mae's daughter. She lived in Seattle and, like Bill, her husband was a Boeing engineer. She had five children. She used a bassinette for her babies that was passed back and forth between her and Betty Hogue, Aunt Nina's daughter. She passed it to me for my babies. My dear Canterbury friend, Betty, the mother of our godson, made a lovely skirt for the bassinette. It was beautiful to be sure, but the offer of such connection with family and with a close friend was even more beautiful.

Aunt Nina wrote assuring me she and Uncle Ray were coming when I got home from the hospital. Aunt Lida sent me the gift of a beautiful bathrobe.

Chapter 15

"Oh, go tell Bill it's a boy." Numbed by spinal anesthetic, I saw the baby held high, supported by the doctor's large hands. He began to cry, and I watched his color change from grayish-blue to light pink, first in the center of his chest then slowly radiating through his body to the tips of his fingers and toes. His bald little head was spattered with blood. His eyes were shut tight to the bafflement of this new world, and his face had a look of outrage and confusion. A nurse wrapped him in a blanket and spirited him away for Bill to see through the nursery window. Bill and I had a brief moment together, and then Bill left for Seattle to see if Mother would come with him to see the baby.

Late in my pregnancy, Mother insisted she was to be with me through my labor. She stated emphatically I could never go through such agony without her presence. We held the position that we would let her know as soon as the baby was born.

"If you don't call me before, then never call me again afterward," she threatened in desperation.

She and Bill came into my hospital room already having seen the baby through the nursery window. I had not seen him since the delivery room.

"How could you do this?" she flayed out at me in a cold fury. "How could you do this?" She kept repeating the question.

"Is the baby beautiful?" I asked her.

"Yes he is, but you certainly are not," she retorted and marched out of the room.

I didn't see Mark until the babies were brought to their mothers at the scheduled time the next morning. I was in a four-bed ward in this small Puyallup hospital. Bill had to leave when visiting hours were over. After the nurse settled everyone for the night, I lay in my bed listening to the quiet breathing of the other women. I threw up after Mother left and felt weak and still a bit nauseous. I closed my eyes, and I could see my baby's face. I dozed on and off through the night, and always my baby's face was right there in front of my closed eyes. I had only seen him in that one brief moment of birth, but I knew him already. I could have picked him out in a crowd of one hundred babies.

In the morning, the doctor discovered I had bled excessively. My blood count had plummeted to a dangerously low level. I was given two units of blood, and the doctor said I was well on the road to recovery.

I was in the hospital four days, and we weren't allowed visitors except husbands and parents. Bill went to work every day and could only come in the evenings. For me, the days were long, especially because the other women had visitors. The baby came four times a day, but he was hardly a visitor.

On the third day, I opened my eyes to see Mrs. Martin standing by my bed. She was carrying a small vinegar cruet filled with tiny garden flowers. She got in by telling the nurses she was Bill's mother. She saw the baby through the window and told me how absolutely adorable and perfect she thought he was. My spirits rose and immediately my body felt strong. I still have that special vinegar cruet.

Aunt Nina was there when we got home from the hospital. By then, she was suffering from breast cancer. Mark was the last new baby she cared for.

Mark was a week old on our first wedding anniversary. Aunt Nina had us pretty much in a routine by then, so she and Uncle Ray went to Seattle to see Mother. Bill cooked a special dinner. I sat at the table with a pillow on the chair, protecting my still sore bottom. But we enjoyed our celebration with Mark in his bassinette beside my chair. Aunt Nina returned to say she had told Mother over and over how well I was doing and what a good mother I was turning out to be. She didn't know if she had convinced her.

Soon it was time to say good-bye to Aunt Nina and Uncle Ray, with hugs and kisses all around. It was hard to see them go, especially because we saw how hard she struggled with the cancer.

"I know I won't make it" she confided in me. "I'm not worried about me, but I do worry about Uncle Ray." We feared we wouldn't see her again, and we didn't. She died in December.

Our new little family of three stayed in our Puyallup home for two more months until our house was ready. It was a good time for Bill and me as we learned to parent a baby. Mrs. Martin was always nearby, as was her daughter who had a baby a few months older than Mark. She regularly stopped by with her baby for visits, and I had a hard time believing that Mark would soon be that big.

I wheeled Mark around town in his buggy doing errands and shopping. People who knew me as a teacher stopped to admire him. Sometimes in the evening, Bill and I drove to the library where we laid Mark on a table as we perused the shelves.

In these early days, I discovered the book, *Baby and Child Care,* by Dr. Benjamin Spock. It was a lifeline then, as it continued to be in the years to come. He inspired confidence, and he provided helpful information on every page. His index was as thorough as an index could possibly be.

One night, Mark finished his late feeding and began to hiccup. When his tummy was full, he fell asleep still hiccupping and continued to peacefully hiccup as he slept. I wondered if something terrible would happen to him if I put him to bed with hiccups and went back to bed myself. I reached for Dr. Spock, and there in the index was "hiccups." I turned to the designated page and read that "newborns often have hiccups even when they are sleeping, and it is nothing to worry about." Soon, I was peacefully asleep myself.

We bought a washing machine and a dryer out of my last paycheck. When Mark was fussy and a load of clothes was drying, I wrapped him in a blanket and put him on the dryer. The vibration and the sound of the motor usually lulled him to sleep.

"What is happening with your mother?" I know you are asking.

We heard nothing from her for a month, and then she called and invited us for dinner. It was like her previous outbursts and attitudes had never happened. She was glad to see us and thought Mark was wonderful.

"Boys are easier than girls," she asserted. "But I don't want him to call me Grandma," she stated emphatically. I was so glad she was seeing us again that I would have settled for him calling her any name.

"Should he call you Lucille?" I ventured.

"Yes, that would be fine." She closed the subject.

When Mark began to talk, he shortened it to Cele, and Cele she became to Mark and all her grandsons yet to come.

Finally, our house was ready and moving day came. "Bring the baby and sit on the porch. You shouldn't be involved in this confusion," insisted Mrs. Martin. Bill supervised the movers who were loading furniture and box after box of everything else. We sat and drank tea while I fed the baby.

The moving van left. Bill and I walked through the empty rooms and then closed the door behind us. I held Mark in my arms as we drove out of town, up Highway 99, and across the floating bridge to our new home. My eyes filled with tears. I looked over at Bill. Tears were streaming down his face as he drove.

Chapter 16

We were in the house two weeks before Bill's parents came for visit. The pace and intensity of my life was catching up with me. I was still tired from the baby's birth and his early weeks as well as from the move itself. I was anxious and apprehensive about the visit. I still missed Aunt Nina and Mrs. Martin. School was starting, and I missed my competency as a teacher. Bill was so eager to show his parents his son and the new house. They insisted that Bill take his two-week vacation while they were there.

Of course, Bill's mother got off the plane talking, and she talked every waking minute she was with us. There were many waking minutes as she had trouble sleeping. She never went to bed before 11:00. So we played bridge every evening. I managed to care for the baby during the hands I was dummy. Bill immediately began a series of migraines that added to my worry, stress, and absence of sleep.

"This house is what we call a project," she announced, referring to housing projects springing up after the war. "It isn't even finished." This was in reference to the unfinished basement. When I was away at the grocery store, she rearranged a kitchen cupboard. She told me the silver serving bowls her friends had sent us as wedding gifts needed polishing, and she pointed out all the baby clothes that needed to be washed by hand. I felt like I was struggling in quicksand.

They liked to have a cocktail or two at 5:00, usually two. "You can't walk on one leg," was how Bill's mother put it. I began to live for 5:00. One night I tried to give in to my fatigue, explaining I wasn't feeling well and was going to bed early. "If you were well enough to have a drink before dinner, you are well enough to play bridge," she said, closing the subject.

On days between headaches, I saw how anxious Bill was to spend time with his father. They stayed out of the house for long periods. They watched the construction workers building homes in the neighborhood, and they dragged home the scrap lumber. They hung out in the garage and storeroom arranging and rearranging the lumber and doing I know not what else. They appeared at cocktail time.

Finally, everyone was so restless that Bill suggested a two-day sightseeing trip to the ocean and around the Olympic Peninsula. We had a brand-new station wagon, which replaced Bill's old Plymouth sedan in which we courted and honeymooned. Mother decided she could leave her job for two days and came along as well. We loaded the car, put Mark in his car seat in the space we called the way back, and off we went.

Bill's father was enchanted with the scenery, which was so different from the East Coast. He sat in the front street with Bill as they continued to enjoy the new station wagon. I sat in the back seat between the other two women.

On a stop overlooking the ocean. We got out for Bill's father to take pictures. As he took a picture of Bill and me standing together, panic filled my entire being. That unreal, disconnected feeling was consuming me. As I had learned in boarding school, I managed not to let on to anyone what was happening to me. I got back in the car, checked on the baby, and off we went. After a while, the panic changed to a feeling of exhaustion.

Following a restaurant dinner where I managed to get a bottle warmed for Mark, we settled into a motel. Mother insisted she stay with the baby so the four of us could have our nightly bridge game.

I was not in charge of my own life. I was not in charge of my own baby. I was a nurse and a maid to my own husband. "It's only for two weeks," Bill responded when I confronted him when we were finally alone in bed.

Later in their visit, Mark was baptized in Christ Church, which was still our church home.

William Marklove, I baptize thee in the name of the Father, and of the Son, and of the Holy Spirit.

I stood at the font with the other two William Markloves, and both our mothers, and our friends, including Mark's godparents. As the priest poured the water over Mark's head and prayed these words, I prayed for a way out of this tight, controlling web in which we were all trapped. We needed one another so very much. I thought there must be a way to make this work.

Friends came to our house for refreshments after the church service. They were eager to see the baby up close and inspect our new home. Mother acted proud to show us off. It was as if we were all her idea, and she was in her own home.

As the two weeks neared an end, Bill's mother took me aside, saying, "Dad and I are so worried because Billie is working nights." Bill was scheduled for a period of working a 3:00 PM to 11:00 PM engineering shift at Boeing. We thought this came at a good time because it would give us time together during the day to get the house more settled, and it would give Bill more time with Mark.

"Successful businessmen don't work swing shift," she warned. "You must talk to Billie about this, as it needs to end."

"Is this how she treats Bill's father?" I thought. I realized with horror that it was.

At last, they were gone, and we reclaimed our home. I put the kitchen cupboard back in order, and Bill restocked the wood in the storage room. Bill indeed did work swing shift. This gave him more time during the day to enjoy Mark and get us completely settled in the house. I was delighted with his company as I embraced and embellished the very first house I could remember. Bill worked overtime through Thanksgiving weekend, and we used the money to buy draperies for the house. At Christmas, our tree reached the ceiling and was topped with a glittering star. A holly wreath graced the front door, and clusters of fat candles glowed on our new marble coffee table. All of this, and Mark dressed in red sleepers with a red Santa hat to match. Like my first Christmas twenty-four years ago, his baby self reveled in the lights and the colors and was so cute as the center of attention. I bought a manger scene, and it occupied a place of honor on the living room mantle. Such was the beginning of our own Christmas traditions.

Soon we began to know our neighbors who were also settling into brand new homes. Like Bill, many of the husbands were Boeing engineers, and they formed carpools for the drive to work. After they left and the schoolchildren were on the school bus, the wives often had coffee gatherings in someone's kitchen with babies on their laps and small children playing nearby. I instantly belonged in this settled, predictable new world with its sense of place, a house, a neighborhood, a husband, and father—a home of our own.

Chapter 17

We lived in what we would always call our Robinswood house for nineteen years. In the next nine years, three more sons were born—your grandsons. Philip Edwin, named after you, was born two years after Mark. After nearly three years, along came Andrew Fredrick, named after Uncle Freddy and my college friend Fred, who became his godfather. John Elliott, the baby of the family, made his appearance four and a half years after that.

"Does anyone have red hair?" I know you are asking. No, your mother's red-haired genes did not continue. Mark, Andrew, and John are blondish, and Philip has dark hair and looks very Welsh like his father. I know your next question. "Didn't you want a girl?" No, there had been such a dearth of men in my life that I felt I was anointed to give birth to boys.

Of course, I knew nothing about raising boys. Dr. Spock's book continued to be my closest companion. In a careless moment, I forgot to put it back, high on the shelf. One-year-old Andrew tore it up and chewed it to pieces. While grieving the original, I promptly replaced it with a new one that I was always careful to put away.

The living room window was behind the Robinswood house and framed the lake and mountain views. In the front, a cozy family room connected at a right angle to the kitchen. Between the kitchen and family room, there was often a playpen for the newest inhabitant. Bill put in a lawn and organized a volunteer work party to pour a cement patio while I planted bulbs and flower seeds.

As babies turned into boys, we added a sandbox, swing set, and a rope swing that hung from a large tree. As the boys grew bigger, the house seemed to grow smaller, and we finished the daylight basement. The house burgeoned with perpetual life and activity.

The boys didn't know that I knew nothing about raising them. That was another one of my secrets. When they look back now, they remember me as all-knowing, all-powerful, and when I shouted, I was a hurricane force to be reckoned with. When I think back on those years now, I remember spanking bottoms too readily, sometimes with the dreaded pancake turner.

Mark struggled with school, and I was too quick to side with the teachers who proclaimed that he was careless and lazy. I was invested in my illusion that I was always right, that I had to be right. I seemed to need this illusion to keep me going.

On the other hand, there were many good times. I delighted in each boy's unique personality and attributes. I relished watching them grow, a virtual garden of boys growing into men, each with unique interests, skills, and struggles. They grew up so fast, before I had learned how to raise them. How I wish you could have been there to be their grandfather.

A rockery in the yard across the street captured my view from the kitchen window. It was planted with seasonal perennials that came into bloom at regular intervals over the entire year. As I worked in the kitchen and looked up to see the rockery, I enjoyed the predictable flowerings and unconsciously began to look forward to what was to come next in the familiar cycle. The plantings started out as little shoots, and in a few seasons, grew to mature plants, now sprawling over the rocks.

One spring morning after we lived in the house five years, I was making coffee and pouring juice as I glanced out the window. "Oh, look; it isn't spinning anymore." My unwashed face with early morning eyes widened, captured by these words I said to myself. The realization flooded me with awe. I stopped and gazed at the rockery just beginning its spring bloom. Where did these words come from? What did I mean, it isn't spinning? It had been a thing of beauty regularly and predictably but often unconsciously in my life for five years. But like the rest of my life, it had been what I best describe as spinning—never still, never being there long enough to allow me to focus. As the boys clamored for their breakfast, I continued to gaze out the window in awe. Like the rockery, my life was no longer spinning.

Soon after we settled in the house, we found a church, a small mission congregation with a backbone of middle-agers supporting a new body of young marrieds, with babies and small children. Before long, we were part of a young couples' group and met, children and all, in various homes for potluck dinners.

There was a beauty of holiness in the Sunday service, even though the small, overflowing baby nursery directly below the sanctuary was staffed by two inexperienced teenage girls. Babies let out loud shrieks regularly during the service. Mothers, each recognizing her particular baby's cry, leaped up and dashed out, no matter if it was during the prayers or in the middle of the sermon.

But one Sunday evening, we were invited to hear a visiting priest. His dark crew cut was etched with gray, and he looked quite conventional in his black suit and round white collar. But when he spoke, he was far from conventional.

He told of receiving a personal Pentecost, what he described as a Baptism of the Holy Spirit, and he spoke in tongues as the Spirit gave him utterance. I quickly moved from interest to fascination to fear to terror. I was overwhelmed with the feelings of the Minneapolis Bible School when I was nine.

But this was my Episcopal church, where I fled at the age of twelve. A church where power such as this was contained in predictable clergy, familiar liturgy, and the power of words, gesture, and movement were safely contained behind altar rails. I encountered a reality that I had successfully buried for seventeen years. When one young woman in the parish was admitted to the hospital with manic delusions, I was even more terrified. I knew the raw power of Pentecost but feared it would drive me insane. The church community was never the same. Soon we stopped talking about what happened. So I had one more secret in my powerful struggle to suppress my own reality.

"It is important that you be an immaculate housekeeper," Mother announced when she cast her eyes around our home. I remember Aunt Lida saying how she complained about housework tiring her to the point that you hired a maid. But in my home, I found her vacuuming, dusting, polishing mirrors, and washing windows, carefully going over the places she thought I missed. "You don't want the house to look like children live here," she muttered.

"You are the center of my life," she declared. "I don't want to be friends with old people and people that don't have husbands." I longed for her approval, her recognition of me as a competent woman, but instead she was only content when she defined and smothered me.

I learned to drive because this was a necessity in our suburban life. I was afraid of driving outside our immediate area, but I got us to the grocery store, cleaners, doctors, dentists, and the boys' schools and activities. I was phobic about driving on the highway and most especially across the bridge that connected Bellevue with Seattle. My phobias plagued me, but with our station wagon filling up with children, I got around for the family essentials.

We made several trips to New York to visit Bill's parents. I liked being in the house where Bill grew up. The boys played with a few very old but fascinating toys they had saved from when Bill was a child. In fact, the house was a virtual museum. They had saved many things from Bill's early years, including his baby teeth, which were carefully counted and placed in an envelope in the top drawer of a dresser.

Always, I encountered Bill's mother's possessiveness of Bill and now creeping possessiveness of the children. If she were challenged in any way, there was the venom of her tongue to reckon with. I especially was the enemy. I learned from Bill and held on to the thought that it was only for two weeks, and many evenings I lived for the cocktail hour.

The years we didn't visit them, they came to see us. During these visits, I had glimpses of how deeply Bill's father cared about the boys. One morning as they were preparing to leave for the airport for their trip home, he sat at the kitchen table holding two-year-old Philip on his lap. He didn't know I was watching as I saw tears streaming down his face. It is a memory I treasure.

When Mark was a year old, we stopped in Minneapolis to see Blanche and Freddy. As I filled her small house with my husband and baby, Blanche seemed overwhelmed. I sensed her unhappiness that she didn't have grandchildren of her own.

"You aren't my girl anymore." she mused. It was true; I wasn't a girl. I was a married woman, and Bill and I slept in the bed where I read *Gone with the Wind* late into the night during a girlhood visit.

"Oh Blanche, I will always be your girl," Not daring to say it out loud, I spoke this reverently inside myself as if it were a prayer.

One day, when we were driving to the doctor for the checkup required to start kindergarten, Mark surprised me by asking, "How did your father die?"

I struggled to come up with a simple explanation. "He got sick with TB and that made him die." In silence , we waited at a stoplight. I looked over and saw that he was pale, with a frightened look in his eyes.

"Am I going to die?" he managed to ask. His voice was so soft I could hardly make out his words. I was struck with horror. I thought I could protect my children from ever fearing in this way. A new baby brother and beginning real school for the first time was a lot for a five-year-old to handle all at once. But remembering my own terror of dying when I was twelve, I sensed that his fear was a reflection of something deeper.

"No way," I managed to respond. "Now they have medicine for TB and nobody dies." I was not sure he was totally convinced.

We moved to a new Episcopal church developing right in our community, close to home. I was glad to be leaving the confusion and turmoil in our former church. I had yet to acknowledge the confusion and turmoil in my own heart that couldn't be fixed by changing churches.

This congregation had just moved from temporary quarters in a school gymnasium to a brand-new building, a sanctuary and parish hall combined in one large space. After the church service, we all moved to the back for coffee hour. The children ran and played while the adults socialized. One morning, I looked up from my coffee and conversation and saw Andrew and two of his little friends walking along the altar rail as if it were a balance beam.

Bill was invited into the newly formed choir. An additional building was completed with classrooms for Sunday school. Remembering the nurturing of my spirit, the beauty of holiness in the Minneapolis Congregational Church when I was a child, I was determined to repeat this for my children and for all the children for that matter. I all but lived in the church nursery or Sunday school.

Chapter 18

"The President of the United States has been assassinated."

It was November 22, 1963, and we sat in horror, riveted to the television as this tragic event unfolded. Mother had always disapproved of President Kennedy. In the first place, he was young. If that weren't enough, he was a Democrat and also Catholic—not our kind of people. His wife wore short skirts and was seen in the newspaper leaving church wearing a sleeveless dress with no hat or gloves.

But Mother stayed with us, seemingly glued to the television First, there was Jackie Kennedy in her blood-spattered suit accompanying her husband's body back to Washington, first to the White House; then in the next three days, to the Capitol where he lay in state; and then to the cathedral for his state funeral. We saw her standing erect outside the Capitol holding the hands of her two small children as her husband's casket passed by.

"Mrs. Kennedy actually plans to walk behind her husband's casket along the route from the Capital to the cathedral." The television announcer shook his head in admiration as he relayed this news. Mother gasped and turned to me. The moment is etched in my memory. I was holding Andrew in my arms. She looked at me and struggled for words.

"Your generation is so amazing and so strong," she blurted. She turned to look at Bill, sitting on the couch with one arm around Mark and the other around Philip. Then, silent once more, she turned back to the television. For that moment, she connected with me in a way she never had before and never would again. It was a moment precious beyond price and a memory I hold forever.

Jackie Kennedy did indeed walk the route from the Capital to the cathedral, and when the service ended, she stood outside and prompted her tiny son to salute his father's casket as it went by. My heart swelled with pride. Would I have been able to do that? How I longed to be strong and brave. Yes, in my mind, Jackie Kennedy knew how to raise a son.

Chapter 19

One day, while shopping, as Andrew sat in his seat in the grocery cart, I turned into the next aisle of the store. Four-year-old Philip had run ahead and stood beside a bin of frozen Popsicles. He looked terrified. I rushed to kneel down beside him. His little body trembled as I put my arm around him.

"My goodness, what's the matter?"

"I'm going to die," he whispered. I was too startled to be afraid. "I ate that," he managed to whisper, pointing to the frost that had collected around the side of the bin. He had broken off a piece, eaten it, and was terrified this impulsive act would cause him to die. I was limp with relief.

While other shoppers pushed around us and Andrew went from fussing to falling asleep in the cart, I managed to reassure Philip. "That is just ice; it won't hurt you." I knelt on the floor holding this desperate child close to me. Finally, fully recovered, he selected a box of animal crackers for the ride home and seemed fine. But I was not. To me, his fear seemed strange and excessive.

Soon Philip developed a fear of going to preschool. "It might burn down," he insisted. Stricken with dread and horror, I felt the worst had happened; he was developing terrors and phobias like I developed as a child and still carried with me.

Then one day as Philip sat on the toilet he began to cry. "If I poop, will I die?" he asked as the tears ran down his cheeks.

"We need a child psychiatrist," I told the doctor. Clad only in his little underpants, Phil sat too quietly on the examination table playing with the stethoscope as we talked.

"It may come to that" he replied. "But I took a special course in emotional problems of children, and I think I can help you. This is all about you, not about Philip."

This was the first time we had seen this doctor. I chose him because he went to our church and sang in the choir with Bill. He was forty years old, seasoned, and mature in my thirty-year-old eyes. I thought he would know where to refer us. He would know what to do.

"I don't want to send you to a psychiatrist. This will label the child in an unfair way. You are a smart and capable mother, and I will help you help Philip get over this." Tall and slender, with a kindly, thoughtful face beneath a balding head rimmed with graying hair, he resembled your picture in an uncanny way. "You're a beautiful young woman," he reflected. "You need to know this." I knew the classes I took at college and my teaching experience did not agree with any of this assessment, but they all seemed to have happened a long time ago in a different life.

He became the children's doctor, but he also became our friend. We soon learned that he was divorced and had small children who lived in another state. He spent a lot of time in our home, enjoying the boys and watching TV with Bill. The boys began to call him Uncle. He drank coffee at the kitchen table with me, telling me about his life and his loneliness. "Find me a wife, just like you," he repeatedly said. If Mother were there, he ignored her. This disturbed her to no end.

The preschool teacher worked with me, helping Philip with his terrors, and with patience and extra attention to his fears, they went away. But secretly I fell in love with the doctor. He was more eager to spend time with me than with Bill. I was flattered that he confided his life history and his own struggles and fears to me.

He knew my worries about Phil's fears and Mark's fears about getting TB, but at office visits, he didn't ask how the children were doing in these areas. He prescribed medicine for their sore throats, stitched up their cuts, and gave them their shots. Each visit, he told me how well I mothered the boys and assured me that I was a good and beautiful woman. I couldn't tell him of my secret fears and phobias and how I lived in terror of passing them on to the boys. His image of me was so flattering I couldn't bear to disturb it. I decided if I worked hard, I could come to believe in his image, live up to it, and all my secrets would just go away.

I looked in the mirror and could see what he meant when he said that I was beautiful. The pregnancies had agreed with me. My too-skinny body had settled into attractive curves just right for my tall frame. I began to appreciate my red hair, the legacy from your mother. I turned to Bill with this new confidence. Although I was conscientiously taking the newly available contraceptive pill, soon our fourth son was on the way.

John Elliott was born unexpectedly, a month early, on Christmas Eve morning. I left Bill and Mother with the boys and Christmas as I rushed to the hospital and spent four glorious days quietly in the hospital with this new son. I managed to keep the doctor; he became John's godfather.

John was an adaptable baby, bouncing along with us to the boy's school, Scouts, music lessons, and church activities. By this time, Mark was nearing junior high school. Philip now insisted on being Phil, and Andrew became Andy. Bill and I said good-bye to our carefully chosen names.

Bill was enjoying increasing responsibility at Boeing, specifically in the design of the electrical system for a new wide-bodied, jet-propelled passenger airplane Boeing was developing. I still liked to remind Bill about your seeing an airplane overhead for the first time when you joined the army. You never could have predicted the development of air travel. Within the next six years, Bill was promoted to a management position. He was affirmed and exhilarated by his work. It grew to involve some travel for meetings with representatives of companies supplying parts for the airplane. He also met with representatives of airlines as they customized the orders for new planes.

He enjoyed this travel because it ran the gamut from Rockport, Illinois, to New York, New Jersey, and Connecticut, along with trips to Japan and France. He thrived on the association with the variety of people that this work provided. Although Bill later worked on several other developing airplanes over the years, he still refers to the 747 as "my airplane." It was there that he came into his own.

These promotions also meant an increasingly larger paycheck. Bill bought a Mustang convertible, abandoning the neighborhood carpool to drive to work every day. Our lives were changing and expanding. For me, caring for John was my easiest job, an interlude of returning to the familiar and a highlight of every busy day.

I threw myself into these increasing demands of marriage and mothering, and this required vast reserves of time and energy. Church required the same but with little payoff. I felt guilty, as if I personally wasn't doing enough to make the beauty of holiness happen for my sons as it had happened for me as a child in Congregational Sunday School. During the rare times I was in church for an entire service, I felt angry. And then I felt guilty for feeling angry, and then I felt angry for feeling guilty.

The liturgy was dead and increasingly long and wordy. The beauty of holiness became so much to dust or so much to pay for as the church budget was always in crisis. Very privately, deep inside of myself I grieved wildly for the loss of God. Had I lost God somewhere as a price for my new stability?

Did God know where I went to church? Did God know about my restored world, marriage, home, and sons? Did God know of my happiness, all that was central to me now? Did God know of my secret disturbing love for the children's doctor? And did God know of a despair looming on the horizon?

Mother's demands and fury were becoming such that I knew she could not have a central place in my life. I could no longer escape the reality that my dreams and efforts were not working, and I couldn't bear it. I stopped going to church.

Chapter 20

I waited in the barbershop, holding John on my lap. By this time, he was an active toddler. We slowly turned the pages of *The Big Picture Book of Things That Go* as the three older boys sat in rows of barber chairs having their crew cuts shorn. As John paused at a page, enthralled with Huckle the Cat going down the fire pole to drive the fire engine to the big fire, I looked up and watched a priest come in the shop, walk across the room, and take his place in the remaining barber chair.

Tall with long legs, he wore the classic black suit and round collar of the clergy. Around his neck was a large silver cross. His mustache matched his light reddish hair, which was graying at the temples. I knew he had to be the new priest in another Episcopal church not far away. From Episcopal scuttlebutt, I had heard that he was filled with the Holy Spirit and how he had received the gift of tongues in a prayer group with that priest who had terrified me earlier.

From my safe, anonymous spot, I watched him with frank curiosity. He closed his eyes as he was draped with the barber cloth, and he looked so still. He seemed to sink into the moment, resting through the haircut that was followed by a careful mustache trim.

"How is it going at your church?" the barber asked, impatient with attempts to draw him into conversation.

"We're building a new one," he opened his eyes, smiled gently in reply, and then returned to his resting pose. This was my first experience of the Reverend Wallace Bristol, Father Bristol, who would become priest, mentor, and friend to Bill and me and to so many others for over forty years.

John grew impatient so I quickly turned the page and directed his attention to Lowly Worm riding in the back of the fire engine, wearing his signature green hat with the yellow feather. The boys' haircuts were still in progress. I continued to watch the priest in the fourth chair. How I longed for his stillness, the deep centeredness that I saw and even felt spilling over to me. Oh, to be at home in the full presence of the Holy Spirit. Like the prophets in scripture who longed to see the face of God and live, I longed to see the face of God and not go insane.

It took me several weeks to muster the courage, but finally I made an appointment and went to talk to this priest. The church building was a former barracks from World War II, and his office was an adjacent portable classroom. Across the parking lot, I saw the emerging structure of a new building. Indeed a new church was being built, literally as well as figuratively. I was terrified I would be a bother, and he would be hurried, busy, or unable to understand why in the world I was there, or he would ask me to teach Sunday school.

"How about a cup of coffee?" he asked. These were his first words after greeting and directing me to a comfortable but well-worn chair. As he poured coffee, I looked around the room. A picture on a nearby wall was unmistakably Jesus, but not a stylized, classical painting of Jesus like those familiar to me. Seated with large open hands resting on his knees, the very human hands of a worker, such as a carpenter, he leaned slightly forward as if speaking intimately to someone.

As Father Bristol and I sipped coffee, I glanced repeatedly from him to the picture and back again as I poured out my life story.

"You need to cry," he reflected as I spoke of the fatigue, anger, guilt, emptiness, and grief that were consuming me. I couldn't do that yet. I didn't tell him I was in love with the children's doctor. To me, then, this seemed like too great a sin to reveal to anyone, especially a priest. Two hours later, I was finished. He invited me to attend Wednesday morning services of Eucharist, Laying on of Hands, and charismatic healing prayer. Coffee, Bible study, and conversation with a welcoming accepting group of women followed the service. And a paid childcare provider was included for the whole morning. I found a community grounded in the grace of God and the presence of the Holy Spirit. The liturgy became alive for me, and this cramped, shabby church bloomed with a beauty of holiness that transcended the environment.

Although these Wednesday mornings became central in my life, I began to rejoin Bill at our other church on Sundays. However, I extracted myself from the children's activities and remained in church for the entire service.

On Maundy Thursday, there was an evening service of Eucharist to commemorate Jesus' last supper with his disciples before his crucifixion. As I sat quietly, listening to the scripture and immersed in the beautiful music, I looked up and saw a vision. I saw a brown rope with a large, shiny hook on the end hooked tightly to another rope. The two ropes extended tightly across the chancel in front of the altar, jarring and disturbing this sacred space.

As I continued to look at the hooked-together ropes, not comprehending what I was seeing, I saw a small luminous figure scrambling back and forth on the ropes, balancing as if on a tightrope. Finally, the luminous figure stopped at the hook. It grabbed the other rope and pulled it hard with both hands. The other rope stretched forward enough so the ropes could be unhooked. As the ropes unhooked and separated, the vision ended, and I was again looking into the familiar span of the chancel. Frightened as I was, I couldn't deny what I had seen.

Church seemed to go on forever, but finally it was over. As an Altar Guild member, it was my job to take home the altar cloth to wash and iron it. I found it covered with wine. Apparently, the chalice containing the consecrated wine had spilled during the service. I gathered up the soaked cloth and the felt pad underneath and went out to the car to wait for Bill. As I sat cocooned in the darkness, torrential rain beat down on the car, striking the roof with the intensity of primitive drums.

Suddenly I was weeping—I, who had not wept for twenty years, since my tears were stopped by Mother's fury outside her door at the end of that long boarding school corridor. My nose ran freely as tears streamed down my face. I realized I was wiping my nose with the altar linen bunched in a bundle on my lap. I tried to stop, knowing this was inappropriate at best and sacrilegious at worst, but the floodgate of tears was open.

And then, there you were, my human father in the car with me. I felt your presence pressing against the right side of my body near the car door. I knew instantly it was you. I recognized you, your reality, the outpouring of your love along with your own grief as my tears continued to mingle with the consecrated wine of the altar linen. We seemed to stay that way for a long time. Finally, my tears were spent, but I continued to feel you right there with me. Then you were gone.

Bill got in the car and drove us home in the merciful darkness, and the din of rain meant I didn't have to explain my disarray. The next day, Good Friday, I washed and ironed the altar cloth, took it back to the church, where I knelt weeping once more, and gave thanks.

After that, I knew you. You were mine, and I was yours. I experienced a father. I had you again in that time in the car. I knew you owned me still, loving and guiding me, passionate about my life.

Before too long, we changed churches for the last time. My Wednesday morning church became our Sunday morning church as well, and Father Bristol became priest to all of us.

Chapter 21

"It's your fault," Bill's father proclaimed in outrage during the long-distance call. He had called to tell us that Bill's mother had suffered a massive stroke. This stroke followed a lengthy telephone confrontation with us about a time they could visit. The boy's activities, our family vacations, and Bill's work schedule resulted in less tolerance for conforming to their own rigid plans and schedule. As much as we struggled, we found no successful way to negotiate, and finally Bill confronted them directly. Bill's mother never again could speak or walk. His father devoted his life caring for her until she died five years later. He died a year after her death, going to his grave blaming me for her stroke. In his mind, I had taken their son away from them.

We bought a tent and all the trappings necessary for the outdoor life, and our family vacations often included a camping trip. I know how much you liked to go camping, and although Mother complained vehemently, you went on camping trips with Uncle Raymond and Aunt Gertrude before I or their children were born. I was convinced that boys needed to go camping.

Bill did not share the passion of my conviction. While I remembered my disappointment when Mother did not allow me to go to Girl Scout camp because I might get appendicitis, he remembered going to summer camp, being the youngest camper, homesick, missing Brooklyn Dodger baseball games on the radio, and eating food out of cans while his face swelled with poison ivy. Secretly, I think he agreed with Mother that camping is too hard, unpleasant, and unsanitary and that improving one's station in life means that you never have to go camping. Through sheer force of will, I won him over. He referred to me as our family's very own camp counselor.

On a trip to Oregon, we stopped to visit Uncle Raymond and Aunt Gertrude at their vacation cabin on the Umatilla River, not far from

Pendleton. They were delighted to see us, get to know us, and experience our boys and family life up close for these three days. We felt the same. While the three older boys explored the woods, walked the trails, went fishing with Bill, swam in the river, and, best of all, floated on inner tubes splashing and crashing into each other in delight, John and Uncle Raymond became best buddies.

They spent hours together sitting on the riverbank, throwing rocks in the river as John laughed in delight at every splash. Every time Uncle Raymond came out of the cabin, John ran to him, took his hand, and led him to their special spot on the riverbank to throw more rocks. As I watched them together, I realized John was nineteen months old, exactly the same age I was when you died. I wondered if Uncle Raymond realized this as well.

On our last evening with them, as we ate dinner outside on their picnic table, John suddenly stood up in the high chair, and it tipped over, throwing him to the ground. John screamed in pain as blood poured from his chin. Aunt Gertrude ran for a towel to compress the wound. Bill reassured the older boys as I comforted John and assessed the damage. Uncle Raymond stood pale and still as if frozen in place.

John needed stitches in his chin, so Uncle Raymond drove John and me to Pendleton and arranged for his doctor to meet us there. On the forty-mile drive, I held John, wrapped in a blanket as I held the towel on his chin while he was still quietly sobbing. Uncle Raymond looked straight ahead, displaying a tense, worried silence. A very kind doctor met us at his office and put the stitches in John's chin.

When we returned to Uncle Raymond in the waiting room, he was still pale and withdrawn, but as we drove back to the cabin, his pent up emotions poured forth.

"You are not Lucille's girl." He cried. "The way you handle this is remarkable." I was astonished at his outburst. John was my fourth son, and by that time, I was not a stranger to boys needing stitches. "These boys are remarkable. You and Bill are wonderful parents. No, you are not Lucille's girl—you are not Lucille's girl in any way."

His words bathed me in glory. "She couldn't handle things. No, she couldn't handle things. You can handle things," he reflected. I sat in silence as there was no need to say anything.

We left them the next morning in a shower of concern, hugs, and well wishes. When we returned home, I began to experience a new clarity about who I was. I knew deeply that I was more than Lucille's girl. As you came to me in the car in the church parking lot, you came to me again through Uncle Raymond in the darkness of that emergency car trip.

If I wasn't Lucille's girl, suddenly it became important to find out who I was. I searched out a psychiatrist and went into psychotherapy. When I firmly asked the children's doctor for a referral and for his advice about this step I was already determined to take, he hesitated. "You're strong enough to get away from your mother on your own; you just need more faith in God," he protested. "Psychiatrists are too expensive. They don't believe in church and are only for people who are mentally ill." So I got a new doctor for the children, and I got a psychiatrist for myself.

"Just say whatever comes into your mind," the psychiatrist instructed on my first visit. He looked to be in his forties with a stocky build and a fair complexion topped with straight, thinning hair. He always wore a heavy tweed suit. His shoes, polished to a high sheen, looked like an Italian designer made them. We sat in nicely upholstered chairs facing each other. He held a yellow tablet of paper and a pen and usually looked down at them, occasionally writing as I spoke.

"Why don't I have a footstool?" As instructed, I said the first thing that came to my mind. His chair had a footstool and mine didn't. He made a few notes on his pad and said nothing. We went on like this for several sessions with long silences as I inwardly criticized the furnishings in the room, what I interpreted as his arrogant attitude, and most of all, I silently criticized myself. Here I was paying him money while I felt worse instead of better. Perhaps the children's doctor was right. I must be doing something wrong.

Finally, one day, I began to talk about you. Soon I was sobbing uncontrollably. I talked about the stories I had heard about your funeral and how people had never seen so many flowers and all the people that came, all the friends and family who loved you so deeply.

"How could you let them down by dying?" I shrieked. "And how could you do this to a helpless baby? You didn't deserve flowers. I never got flowers. Nobody came to see me. You had the nerve to shut yourself up in a hospital, give up, die, get flowers and adoration, and had a beautiful funeral. And you left me, a baby daughter, to clean up your mess—the havoc you left behind in the issues of your own marriage."

I thought the psychiatrist should be writing all this down on his yellow pad, but he sat there looking down, not writing a word. When he stood up to indicate the session was over, I stood up and kicked the footstool clear across the room before I walked out the door.

When I returned the next week, the footstool was back in its place, and the psychiatrist's countenance was unchanged. I managed to keep the furniture intact as I went on to express my fury to Mother. It was as if she were right there, perched on that footstool along with you.

"I'm not your goddamn husband," I howled at her through the sobs wrenching through my body. "I deserve to be treated like a loving daughter. It was your job to love me, nurture me, and then let me go." The feelings continued pouring out. My soul was erupting like a volcano. "You had a husband for thirteen years. You knew him. I never had a father. Leave me alone and get on with it. Stop trying to live a perverted, stunted life using me as your crutch." She felt like an attacking monster and with a superhuman force I didn't know I possessed, I shook her off my back if she were really that attacking monster.

I went home from these sessions and cried even more. When the older boys were in school and John was down for his nap, I sobbed. That was my crying hour. I sat at the kitchen table, my cup of tea untouched, as waves of grief so strong I feared they would break me into pieces poured over me. At last, I grieved your death. It wasn't Mother's grief, Aunt Lida's grief, or Uncle Raymond's grief; it was my grief that I experienced at last. And gradually I began to feel stronger.

I noticed my agoraphobia was gone. My fear of going insane was gone. I could drive on the freeway and over bridges all over downtown Seattle totally calm. A new world opened up for me.

Although Bill was reluctant to take on any more conflict after his parent's tragic reaction to his developing autonomy, he got behind me when we confronted Mother. We stopped making her demands the center of our attention and plans. When decisions were made about visits back and forth or holiday plans, we expressed our own feelings and priorities.

"I am going to die," she proclaimed, but we held to our convictions. She never forgave me. Hurling accusations that I was uncaring, unappreciative of her sacrifices, self-centered, unloving, and mentally unstable, she shut herself up in her apartment and had as little as possible to do with us from then on.

This new stance we took had a ripple effect on some of our oldest friends. Their backgrounds, drastically different from ours, became starkly apparent. We couldn't find words to talk about the hidden anguish we were going through with both sets of parents. As we distanced ourselves from one another, it felt as if we were losing brothers and sisters as well.

But we noticed new friends around us. Our Saint Margaret's community, still centered in what I called my Wednesday morning church, expanded into Sunday morning church with its energetic throng of worshipers. Many were families with children about our age. Social gatherings spun off from this. Bill joined the choir, and it could be depended on to generate at least two great parties during a typical year. There was a sense of God being very close and with us everywhere, even in the grocery store.

"Is that Jesus?" three-year-old John asked one day as we were shopping and the manager unexpectedly handed me a bouquet of flowers.

The older boys joined Boy Scouts, and their camping skills developed to the point that I no longer qualified as camp counselor. The highlight of their activities were weeklong father-and-son hiking and camping trips. These hikes included excursions to such places as across the Olympic Peninsula and around the foothills of Mt. Rainer. Bill Landon, the Boy Scout leader, became a household name, so important was his leadership in Bill's shared hiking and camping experiences with his sons.

As I helped them pack and get ready for these trips and drove them to the trailheads to meet the rest of the troop, I often thought of you, Dad. Somehow, you seemed very close. I remembered how you enjoyed camping and how much you would appreciate hearing all about these hiking and camping weeks from your son-in-law and your grandsons.

And then there was Seabeck, a family camp at a beautiful conference center on Hood Canal with the Olympic Mountains benevolently in their place in the distance across the water. In the mist of this beauty, we found what quickly became a magical extended family. Every year, the last week in July became Seabeck week.

The week included dynamic speakers and programs, special activities for children and teenagers, sports competitions, swimming, fishing, square dancing, but most importantly, it included everyone simply being with one another. We became part of this group of families who returned each year. To this day, we refer to the Seabeck community as our other church. It is extended family as well, with aunts, uncles, and cousins for our sons.

"Why can't Cele come to Seabeck with us?" Andy asked when he noticed that some families included grandparents.

"I don't know," was the best I could reply. In such dramatic ways, our lives had moved on without her.

Year 'round friendships developed from the Seabeck week. My self-image soared when I was invited to be part of a women's bridge club that met the first Monday evening of each month. Boldly leaving husbands to deal with anything going on in the family, bridge night was sacred. It included at least as much talk as it did bridge playing, and wine glasses were replenished regularly during an evening that often extended beyond midnight. Sharing in the experiences of these other sensitive and accomplished women also with marriages and families with emerging teenagers was calibration for me as I felt my way in my own life.

Bill and I were part of a group of parents that coordinated youth activities at church. We planned programs and outings, chaperoned dances and excursions, slept in sleeping bags at conference centers or on church floors, and for those times, were absorbed with the energy and challenges of teenagers. "Think of how God felt halfway through creation," I whispered to Bill during the times he longed for nothing more than a cold martini and his own bed.

Chapter 22

"I want to go back to school." I broached the subject with Bill as we sipped martinis at a restaurant on a night out just for us. "If you and the boys help more around the house, and if we have a cleaning lady once a month for thorough housework, we can make this work." I plunged on with my proposal. Bill looked at me in total bafflement.

"Why aren't you happy just being at home, now that the boys are older," he pondered.

"You are thirty-nine years old. Why in the world do you want to go to school, of all places?" But as busy as he was in his work and with his activities with the boys, he saw that I was serious, and he agreed to get behind this project and make it work. So I went back to school.

My routine changed dramatically. I gave up Wednesday morning church. It had been a central source of spiritual nourishment and nurture for such a long time. But I could now bear to let it go. I remained on Altar Guild for Sunday morning church, and Bill and I continued helping with the teenagers.

I was accepted into a program at the University of Washington that would lead to a master's degree in speech and language pathology. When he was nine, Andy struggled with stuttering in his speech. I tried to learn ways to help Andy through this from the school speech pathologist, and I wanted to learn more. But I learned much more than that.

School was difficult and demanding. I had not studied like this for seventeen years. My life had been a multitasking one, listening and screening in or out many voices at once. Now my job was to attentively listen to one voice—a lecture—take notes, study these notes intensely, and then take a test on the material. During classes, I had a tendency to think about the boys at home or my grocery list or how many clean socks Bill had in his drawer before I needed to do laundry. Many of the students were twenty-three years old, just out of their undergraduate work, and their listening skills were focused and still well-honed.

But at the same time, school was exhilarating. In addition to our coursework, we studied neurology, anatomy, and physiology. The complexity of the human body was new to me, like unlocking a mysterious foreign language. We dissected larynxes and lungs of cadavers in the medical school's anatomy lab. Then there was the moment I held a human brain in my hand. As I turned it carefully studying its size, shape, color, and texture, its grooves of interconnecting pathways, each with its function yet designed to work in synergy with one another, I remembered the words from a Psalm: "Oh God, I am fearfully and wonderfully made."

We moved on to do practicum in the speech clinic, working with patients with many types of disorders and challenges. It was healing and mending work with the human nervous system. For me, it was prayer.

"How is your mother doing?' I know you are asking me, Dad. I tried phoning her periodically in an attempt to establish some contact, but all I heard were long sighs and silences, and my attempts at conversation were not successful. Then, when I was at the university, I established a pattern of stopping by her apartment once a month. I rang the doorbell, and she let me in. She sat in silence as I talked about the family's current activities and about my university life. Periodically she sighed. This was reminiscent of the silent treatment I used to receive as a child when I didn't please her. At that time, after not more than two days of this silence from her, I could tolerate no more and did anything she asked. But those days were over.

My best image of life with Mother was a fulcrum with one of us at either end. It was my job to keep the fulcrum in balance, like a child's teeter-totter. If she moved forward and I didn't move commensurately, I could crash to the ground. My survival depended on sensing her every move. As I grew older, I systematically weighed in my mind how much out of balance I could tolerate. But now, I got off the teeter-totter, let her down as gently as I could, and walked away. The game stopped, and I longed for something to take its place, but I let go of expectations. I knew it was up to her.

I continued the monthly visits and found her unchanged. She seemed focused on her apartment and continued to be an immaculate housekeeper. She kept simple food in the house to prepare. She bought a television set and watched it most of the day.

The boys shot up like corn in a Midwestern summer sun. On some days, literally, I could watch them grow. Soon Mark and Phil were taller than Bill. Andy was not far behind, and John was in grade school. Mark went off to Central Washington College in Ellensburg. The family was no longer completely contained under one roof. Phil followed in two years to Washington State University in Pullman, where Andy would join him in three years. Girlfriends appeared, some long-term, some short-term, but they showed up from everywhere. After years of only boys and their guy friends in the house, I enjoyed this new dimension in our lives.

We sold the house and moved to a new and larger home not far away. The Robinswood house and its solid neighborhood had done its work. My life had a sense of permanence, and it had stopped spinning. From my kitchen window, I said good-bye to that rockery across the street, still beautiful in each seasonal splendor. It remains firmly in place in my memory. It, too, had done its work.

As Phil finished high school, I finished graduate school and got a job as a speech and language pathologist in the rehabilitation department of Valley General Hospital. To receive certification, I completed a clinical fellowship year preceded by a final examination to determine clinical competence. Because of the demands of family life, I wanted to work half–time, and I was offered the option of doing this.

The information in class notes and textbooks from the graduate program came together as I revisited them after a day of seeing such a variety of patients. And I had a paycheck, small in comparison to what Bill's paycheck had become, but a real paycheck all the same.

After I worked for three years, the hospital sent me for an eight-week training course in neurodevelopmental therapy for infants and children with cerebral palsy. Occupational therapists, physical therapists, and speech pathologists trained together, each with her own specialty. We worked with children during this training but practiced with each other as well, assessing movement and learning techniques to help normalize muscle tone, balance, and movement. I became aware of stiffness, tension, lack of synergy, and balance in my own muscles and nerves, not neurologically based, but consistent with my emotional trauma as a child.

This body awareness, new to me at age 47, was surprising and encouraging. I went on to learn about the Feldenkrais method of awareness through movement. I used these practices to soften and relax my body to move more freely.

I began to love my body even as it was moving into middle age. It was me—separate from Mother, separate from Bill, and separate from the boys. I felt autonomous.

I moved on to work in a coordinated children's therapy program at Good Samaritan Hospital in Puyallup.

"How is Bill weathering all this autonomous body stuff?" I know you are asking. Looking back, I wonder as well.

Mark and Phil were nearly through college, and Andy, a high school senior, was on his way out of the nest as well. John was in junior high school. Even with the dog and the cat, the house was cleaner and quieter. Sometimes Bill and I looked around and wondered where everyone had gone so fast.

Bill continued to have a passion for his work, and he was very good at it. But with each new airplane design, the work became more complicated. New technologies developed every day. In a workday, he attended meeting after meeting with a complex and shifting array of people. This was stressful. In earlier days, there had been a simpler camaraderie in a smaller working group. Since the boys required less of my time, I focused more on my work, and we no longer understood each other's work.

Then there was church. It was changing, and we couldn't connect there in ways we had connected in Canterbury days and earlier times when we were raising the boys at St. Margaret's. Now there was a more informal liturgy, modern guitar music, and women priests. I embraced the changes wholeheartedly. Bill resonated deeply with the old ways and most definitely did not appreciate this drastic newness. So we didn't connect in the automatic ways we had before, and each of us began blaming the other for this unhappiness.

Then we found Bev Gorsuch, an exceptionally wise, skillful, and sensitive counselor. From her, we learned the word *individuation*. Bev used that word so often it began to resonate in our ears. We needed to *individuate,* she explained. Our job was to let our marriage unfold, not to be afraid to allow it to become the very best for us now. Gradually, we began to let each other be. We were two strong people who loved each other so much; we were both afraid of loosing the other as a price for our change and growth. As we practiced, the new ways became more familiar ways. And to Bill's delight, he was assured that I was more than willing to share my new middle-aged autonomous body.

In the midst of the bodywork and the marriage work, I discovered the Progoff Intensive Journal. This loose-leaf notebook with its variety of colored dividers designating the writing work for each section gave me a way to remember and reflect on my life experiences with increasing depth and clarity. I went on to present workshops explaining this kind of journal-keeping and the ways to use it as a developmental tool. The people who came to the workshops inspired my own journal work as well.

Chapter 23

"My bank has moved, and I can't find my money." It had been eight years since I heard Mother's voice on the phone.

"I'll be right over." I managed to keep the surprise out of my voice.

Her nearby bank, where she regularly walked to, had not closed. She simply could no longer find it. Her last two undeposited Social Security checks lay on the table along with her checkbook and a neat pile of unpaid bills.

"It's because the bank moved," she insisted.

"I'll drive you to the bank. We can put my name on your account, and I'll write the checks." I was relieved when she consented to the plan.

I noticed there was little food in the house, so when we left the bank, our mission successfully accomplished, I risked another step.

"Since we are out with the car, let me drive you to the grocery store."

"All right, but you wait here," she insisted as we drove into the Safeway parking lot.

I sat in the car watching her thin, frail body make its way to the store entrance. I waited five minutes then followed her at a distance. I heroically held back tears as I watched her weaving the grocery cart through the aisle. Confused and uncertain, she was quickly tiring as she struggled to find the coffee, bread, cereal, and frozen dinners that had been in the same spots in that store since I was in college.

I managed to show up behind her at the counter as the checker handed her back the $10.00 she had overpaid. She let me carry the groceries to the car and didn't even remind me of the carton of eggs I had carelessly dropped in 1952.

I visited her the next day and found her still cordial and surprisingly open to me. She was glad the bills had been paid.

"Let me help you more," I offered. "We can find you a place to live where your housework will be done and your meals all prepared."

"You mean an old folk's home where everyone is old and everyone is crazy."

As I heroically held back tears in that moment in the grocery store, I managed to hold back a smile as I listened to what was really a disparaging description of herself.

I found a retirement home in Bellevue not far from our house. She consented to a visit, and then protested it was far too expensive, and she wouldn't socialize with all these old people.

"You would have your own little studio apartment and wouldn't have to socialize.

You could sit by yourself during meals."

I could see her doing just that.

Her life became even more difficult in her apartment as she put off the decision to move. I stopped by regularly to pay her bills and pick up the laundry that she finally consented to my doing.

"Be careful. You always ruin everything when you wash it," she cautioned.

I faced the possibility she might stay where she was until she exhausted or injured herself. But I continued to be mindful of the boundaries I needed to maintain between us, lest she still destroy me.

Then Bill had an idea. Mark, a senior at the University of Washington, wanted an alternative to dormitory life. "Would your mother move if she thought she was giving up her apartment for Mark?" he wondered. That's what it took. She agreed to move on the condition that if she wanted her apartment back, Mark would move out. Mark readily agreed to the condition. In the ensuing shuffle of furniture, I had that small desk you gave Mother refinished and moved to a place of pride in our living room.

Mother lived in the retirement home four years. At first, she spent most of her time in her room watching a predictable sequence of soap operas on television. She also watched football games. This surprised me until I remembered her telling me that you and she used to regularly travel to Seattle with a group of friends for the University of Washington Husky' games. She said you personally knew the man who wrote the Husky fight song.

I visited weekly to take her to the beauty parlor. I continued to pay her bills and do her laundry. Gradually, she got used to the people around her and sometimes even ate meals with a cluster of other residents. The staff encouraged her to sit in the lobby or go on outings with the other residents, but she preferred her room with her television for company.

One day, a very large television was placed in the lobby. After lunch, Mother lingered in the lobby more and more often, obviously enjoying this expansive screen.

"Did you know Cele has a boyfriend?" Phil exclaimed. He had stopped to visit her on a semester break from college. I, too, had noticed her often sitting on a couch beside an elderly gentleman. After a few weeks, they were holding hands, both still looking straight ahead, seemingly engrossed in whatever was on the screen. This was causing an obvious stir in the lobby community. Ladies stopped me in the hall either smirking or clucking despairingly.

"Do you know your mother has a boyfriend?" they would ask, rolling their eyes.

Of course, Mother never talked to me about this man, and I knew better than to ask. When I came in, I would stand across the way and watch them benevolently before Mother saw me, pulled away, and stood up. He looked like a very nice gentleman. She was eighty-seven, and I had never before seen her holding hands with a man.

The time came when Mother needed more assistance than the retirement home provided. One day, I found her television set toppled over on the floor, and she didn't know how it got there. Then a spring from the innerspring mattress on her narrow bed came loose, and I saw it poking through the sheet. When I checked her for puncture wounds, she insisted it didn't matter because she just slept on the other side anyway. It was clearly time to move to another level of care. As she became increasingly confused, she became more passive and seemed comfortable now with her dependence on me.

Bill and I moved her to an adult family home, a place for adults with special needs to receive care. Four residents lived there, cared for by a capable lady named Kathryn, who owned the home and lived there as well.

I visited many adult family homes before finally settling on this one. It turned out to be the perfect choice. An experienced friend wisely advised me, "Remember, you are choosing a home for your mother as she is now, not as she was earlier. Remember also that you are putting your mother in someone else's home. You are not in charge of it." This was good advice.

One of the residents, a very ancient man named Ralph, chain-smoked cigarettes and had an equally ancient dog, his beloved friend, that lived in his room. Two cats also romped and played throughout the house. One or the other always ended up on the kitchen counter during their kitty game of King of the Hill. In addition to all this, Kathryn had two teenagers. I could just imagine what Mother would have said about this in an earlier time.

But the cluttered kitchen often smelled like cookies were baking. Mother's room was near the kitchen, where, as Kathryn put it, "I can keep a special eye on her."

Kathryn and I bonded nearly on sight. I watched her with the residents and saw that, along with being very skilled and capable, she genuinely enjoyed and cared about each one and was sensitive to every individual need. And if Ralph burned the house down or the dog infested it with fleas, I was not in charge.

I visited twice a week on my days off from work. Soon I saw that Mother had bonded with Kathryn.

"I like you," I heard her confide to Kathryn, and she actually managed a smile. On my visits, I found myself lingering over coffee and cookies in the kitchen or at the craft table getting to know the other residents and talking woman talk with Kathryn. Or we talked shop because she had formerly worked in a hospital. Sometimes Mother's expression brightened a bit, and she seemed interested in our conversation.

"My daughter never gave me a moment of trouble," she bragged one day. Kathryn and I winked at each other as I basked in the moment.

All of a sudden, it seemed our family was immersed in wedding plans. "Can Cele come to the wedding?" Andy the groom and his bride, Lesley, pleaded. Lesley's grandparents were coming all the way from England, and Andy wanted his only grandparent to be there as well. Kathryn joined in on their behalf. "I can get her ready. All you have to do is pick her up and bring her back."

It was a Christmas wedding, and I bought her a pretty, red wool dress. Kathryn took her to the beauty parlor. Mark escorted her down the aisle, and, to my eyes, she looked lovely. A friend drove her back to Kathryn directly after the ceremony. I have a picture of her amidst the festivities. Even though there is a vacant look on her face, I treasure the picture.

Chapter 24

By early 1985, Mother was noticeably weaker. She usually stayed in bed until midmorning, and then she sat in her chair, a vacant look on her face even as the teenagers' radios played and the other residents chattered at the craft table.

In May, she was diagnosed with cancer. Our family was in the midst of another wedding, this time Phil and his bride, Karen. (Yes, you now have two granddaughters-in-law.) There was no thought of Mother attending the wedding.

I made the decision that she would not have chemotherapy and receive only palliative care. Strangely, she never needed pain medication, only a tranquilizer so she would not be anxious.

One day she resisted the pill Kathryn offered her.

"I don't have to take this because I am leaving soon." Suddenly Mother's voice was strong with an air of dignity and authority Kathryn had not heard before. I remembered this voice well.

"My husband is downtown at a hotel, and he is coming to get me." Kathryn was concerned, and she phoned to tell me about this.

"Nice of him to show up," I muttered, clearly reflecting the strain I was under.

Later in the day, I stopped to visit. She was lying in bed, and when she saw me, she struggled to sit up. I sat on the side of the bed facing her, and put my hands across her back to support her. She looked right at me.

"Raymond and Gertrude are here," she announced. Her eyes widened, and there was excitement in her voice. I shook my head. Uncle Raymond and Aunt Gertrude had been dead for several years. But gradually I recognized what was happening. Insight along with gratitude pounded over and around me like warm ocean waves. Of course Raymond and Gertrude were here. As they had been here for us all of our lives, they would be here now. They were with you at that hotel as you were coming to pick her up.

The next day was my day off from work, but I didn't go back to visit Mother. I left her with you, Uncle Raymond, and Aunt Gertrude in a place that was not for me. I went to downtown Seattle for a therapy appointment with Bev Gorsuch, and then I went to the Pike Place market to have lunch with a friend. When I got home, there was a message to call Kathryn. Gently, she relayed the news. "Your mother has died." She died that afternoon, peacefully as she slept. You had arrived to take her back.

Bill and I took her body to Portland to bury her in the wall in Portland Memorial Mausoleum just down the hall from where your body lies. When I phoned my cousin Faye to tell her we were coming, she invited us to stay and spend the night with them.

The night after she died, when we were still in Bellevue, I sat for a long time in the mortuary beside her body already in its casket. She wore the pretty red dress I bought her for Andy and Lesley's wedding. Mark joined me for a time, bringing a single red rose. Then the casket was closed and a spray of lavender and pink flowers placed on it. The next day, I rode in the hearse with her body carrying Mark's rose. Bill followed in the car.

As we made this three-hour journey, I was aware of its symbolism. It represented you and Mother's journey from your early days at J. A. Campbell Company when you traveled as a salesman from Seattle to Portland, visiting towns along the way. Then from your's and Mother's courtship and marriage in Seattle to your home in Portland when you became regional manager of the Portland office. Then to your trips back and forth to visit the Seattle home office, bringing Mother to parties with other employees and to attend University of Washington football games. Even though we now traveled on a six-lane freeway, the route was so significant for Mother's final journey.

A bevy of cousins were already at the mausoleum to greet us—Bill and Ginny Ralston, Faye and Bill Sabo, and Arlene Hennessy. Of course, Aunt Lida's son, Bill, was thinking about my early years when we lived in their home during your sickness and death. Arlene and Faye were remembering living there too, caring for me. Bill Ralston looked around thoughtfully.

"I remember my mother coming here on the streetcar every week for years bringing flowers." This was precious information to share with me.

The casket was brought in and placed beside the wall. We gathered around as an Episcopal priest read the service of committal from the Book of Common Prayer. The casket was briefly opened as I placed Mark's rose inside. Then it was lifted into its place in the wall.

Bill had thought to bring flowers for your vase, and we walked down the hall and placed them there. We lingered a bit, each in his or her way aware of the significance of these moments. I felt as if I had come to the end of a long journey.

Bill Sabo took us all to a restaurant for dinner. Wine bottles were passed around the table, and my Bill had a martini as well. The next morning, there were hugs all around as everyone came back to the Sabos to see us off for home.

Sons and daughters-in-law were waiting for us when we got home. We had a simple memorial service conducted by Father Bristol in the Saint Margaret's chapel. Mark and Andy played guitars as the four sons and two wives sang a song from the book of Ecclesiastes:

> To every thing there is a season,
> and a time to every purpose under heaven:
>
> A time to be born, and a time to die,
> a time to plant and a time to take up that which is planted;
>
> A time to kill and a time to heal; a time to break down
> and a time to build up;
>
> A time to weep, and a time to laugh; a time to mourn,
> and a time to dance;
>
> A time to cast away stones, and a time to gather stones together;
> a time to embrace and a time to refrain from embracing;
>
> A time to get, and a time to lose; a time to keep,
> and a time to cast away;
>
> A time to rend, and a time to sew; a time to keep silence,
> and a time to speak;
>
> A time to love, and a time to hate;
> a time of war and a time of peace.

I knew all those times. I sat deeply in prayer as the words sung by these precious people reverberated through the chapel. Then I heard still another voice singing with them, a stark high voice weaving into the harmony a pure, ethereal obligato. Was it an angel joining us to fully celebrate a new season, to welcome in this new time, a time of grace?

Epilogue

I wonder if my parents know about Sarah. These thoughts came unbidden and overwhelmed me as, a year after Mother's death, I held my first-born grandchild in my arms. A girl, Sarah Anne, born October 12, 1986, to Phil and Karen, on what would have been your ninety-third birthday. Amid the family members gathered to enjoy this moment, I struggled to hold back tears. I, who had birthed four sons, now held the first child of a brand-new generation, a fresh, tiny new branch on the family tree. It had begun with a girl. I wonder if you and Mother know about Sarah. I think you do.

About the Author

Janet Lloydis a wife, mother, mother-in-law and grandmother. A retired speech-language pathologist and counselor, she is a lay pastoral minister, healing minister and spiritual director at St. Margaret's Episcopal Church in Bellevue, Washington.

Printed in the United States
131083LV00005B/15/P